Love Making His Way

BY LORNE SHEPHERD

FOREWORD BY DAVID MAINSE

ISBN-0-920195-04-0

Copyright © 1985 Lorne Shepherd

Printed in Canada
Harmony Printing Limited
123 Eastside Drive, Toronto, Ontario M8Z 5S5

Published by Little Ones Books
Toronto, Ontario, Canada
Young America, Minnesota, U.S.A.

Contents

Foreword

Lorne Shepherd for 25 years was a full-time television broad-caster. He saw, from the inside, the effects of the media on the human family. He recognized the manipulation and the sub-liminal effects of the omnipresent little screen and he was spurred to read everything available which would provide an alternative for positive and constructive marriage and family relationships.

He has given himself totally to the task of applying the eter-nal principles which he has learned, to the human family. Recognizing this as God's call upon his life, he has left his very successful television career and has devoted himself 100% to serve as the minister to the family for the 100 Huntley Street television ministry.

His days are full with counselling appointments and his evenings and weekends are filled with group sessions or seminars. I have personally met dozens of couples who have told me that Lorne shepherd has been God's means of put-ting them back together again after separation and even after divorce. I've heard others say that Lorne, by his counsel, has turned a bad marriage into a good marriage and a good mar-riage into a better one.

Lorne's wife, Doris, is a department head here at 100 Huntley Street and his son, David, is on our television crew. They are working together in beautiful harmony illustrating the qualities of life which are so important to all of us.

In Christ's Love and Service,

David Mainse
Host of 100 Huntley Street

Introduction

This is a book about love: about relationships between men and women, and the family.

Love is what holds the whole world together in the area of relationships. If a child doesn't receive love in its' early years of life, the child will die. No adult can live without being loved and without giving love. We can never exhaust the subject of love and never minimize its importance.

The world is constantly using a term through television and the printed media of 'making love'. Not one of us has ever made love, because God has made all love. We don't make love! He created in us the ability to love and experience love. The only way we can come into that experience is when we come into harmony with His very nature. When God speaks of Himself He says that *He* is love. He created the whole idea of love, and the relationship aspect is His idea and plan. We can only experience it, His way.

The fact that God is love and He has created us in His image, means that unless we become like Him, we die. We die emotionally, physically, mentally and spiritually. To become like Him is to be *filled* with love. His plan for sharing love with one another is good and He is delighted when we learn His way of loving one another, in *every* area of our life.

This is a book about love, sharing, getting to know one another, the sexuality between a man and woman, in a life-time relationship with God at the center and establishing a loving family and home. If we do not begin now, civilization will crumble around us. As you read this book, ask God to teach you how to love . . . and I know He will answer your prayer.

Chapter One

God's Priorities

This book is not the greatest book on relationships that has ever been written. That volume was completed almost 2,000 years ago, and nothing produced since has ever come close. That's right - I'm referring to the Bible. The Word of God is undoubtedly the most interesting, exciting and relevant book ever written. Our studies in this book will simply act as a guide to key principles in the Bible, principles which, if you follow them, will improve every aspect of your life. As you apply God's directions for living, you will find that your emotions and your attitudes will undergo dramatic changes, and the areas of your life that are confused or crippled will be healed.

My goal, in this book, is to help every reader discover peace and wholeness in areas of his or her life where there have been anxiety and struggle.

"To every thing there is a season, and a time to every purpose under the heaven: A time to be born, and a time to die; a time to plant, and a time to pluck up that which is planted; a time to kill and a time to heal; a time to break down and a time to build up; a time to weep, and a time to laugh; a time to mourn and a time to dance; a time to cast away stones, and a time to gather stones together; a time to embrace, and a time to refrain from embracing; a time to get, and a time to lose; a time to keep and a time to cast away; a time to rend and a time to sew; a time for silence and a time to speak; a time to love and a time to hate; a time of war and a time of peace. What profit hath he that worketh in that wherein he laboureth? I have seen the travail, which God hath given to the sons of men to be exercised in it." (Ecclesiastes 3:1-10 KJV).

The Gift of Time

Time. In this scripture, the writer speaks of a gift shared by each person who is born - the gift of time. We all have a limited number of days and hours in our lives. We also all know that time is going to run out on us, one day. We cannot stop time, and we can do little or nothing to add to the time-span allotted to us.

Everyone, everywhere on earth, has exactly 24 hours in each day. Thus, we are all faced with the challenge: to use this time in the most productive way possible.

Yet it is amazing the way we waste this precious possession. And, don't forget, there are many people out there who have made it their goal to help you waste your time, and even to use time destructively! I have been involved in television for more than three decades, including 25 years in secular television production. I have attended sessions in which the theme of the presentation was how to devise methods, through subliminal influences, to control the viewer's time. Television people are always reaching to grab more of your time. They say, "We're going to have a TV in every room . . . we're going to become a member of this family!" Time is a gift to you, but everyone is trying to gain control of your precious gift, and no one succeeds as well as television!

I am not suggesting that every television producer or director has sinister motives. They are usually following their own philosophy of life, a philosophy known as "secular humanism", which essentially is based on the concept that man can solve his own problems without God. This invariably leads to destruction! The Apostle Paul was writing about such people when he wrote, under the guidance of the Holy Spirit, "For even though they knew God, they did not honour Him or give thanks; but they became futile in their speculations, and their foolish heart was darkened. Professing to be wise, they became fools" (Romans 1:21-22 NASB).

Do you ever waste time? I know that I do. Most of us waste incredible amounts of this valuable commodity. Of course, sometimes it can actually be good to waste time, because it can be a serious affliction to be enslaved by time. We all know folks like that, as well – they are always running to beat the clock,

2

forever checking their watches. Their whole life is planned down to the last second. It seems to me that people in large urban centres, such as Toronto, are especially prone to this disease! and most of us know what it is to be pushed by time, to be on the run, usually to nowhere.

But all of us, whether we are time-wasters, or time-slaves, have only a certain amount of time. The question is, what will we do with it? What are your time-priorities?

Perhaps we can compare it to having money. You determine how, and if, your needs are going to be met, by how you manage your money. You might have a million dollars, but if you spend it all on bubble gum, you'll have a million bucks' worth of bubble gum, but you will starve to death! Some people waste their money in ways almost as ridiculous as that. And a lot more of us waste our time in foolish ways.

There are a lot of areas in our lives which demand sections of our time. High on our list should be "work". The Bible says that if you don't work, you should not eat (II Thessalonians 3:10 NASB). God expects us to provide for ourselves and for those for whom we are responsible. He made us this way. Psychologists say that people who live entirely dependent on the gifts of others become very unhappy. Have you ever noticed that, if someone is continually giving you gifts, but you never have a chance to give anything back, you begin to resent that person? Some people do this to their children. They keep giving and giving and do not allow the child a chance to take responsibility for himself or herself. And then they wonder why the children resent them.

God has constructed us to only feel right about ourselves if we have achieved something, and reaped the rewards of that achievement. Therefore, work is a high time priority in God's plan for you.

Sleep

Can you guess another high priority? Let me suggest: sleep. You have to sleep. Some people try to live their lives so full of other priorities that they never take sufficient time to sleep. I know of one man who sleeps for three hours a day for weeks at a time, and then, after a while, he will "crash out" for a whole day. I am no diagnostician, but my guess is that if he lives past 45, it will be a miracle!

Doctors tell us that the average adult needs seven hours of sleep each night. There is some variation, from person to person, but this is the normal requirement if we are to maintain mental, emotional and physical health. God made us in such a way that sleep has to be a high priority.

Nutrition

"Whether, then, you eat or drink or whatever you do, do all to the glory of God" (I Corinthians 10:31 NASB). For a lot of us, this third priority is our favourite: eating. God has made us so that we need to have regular meals. In our day, many of us live our lives on the "eat and run" style, but this can be just as dangerous as living on little or no sleep.

Relationships

"It is not good for the man to be alone" (Genesis 2:18 NASB). These first three priorities are obvious, and although you may be bending God's plan by ignoring sensible patterns of working, sleeping and eating, you are probably finding time for each of them somewhere in your life. But many of us ignore some of God's other time priorities for our lives. A most important priority in His plan for us is: relationships.

For a lot of you, your closest relationship is with your spouse. Yet many people in our day are totally ignoring the development of this relationship. We take our spouse for granted, and then we are astounded when we no longer have a spouse! This occurs in many of our other relationships, with family and friends, as well. It takes time for a love relationship to develop, time "focused" specifically on that relationship. If you do not invest the necessary time, there will simply be no relationship!

Communion with the Father

Here is another time priority that may not appear on a lot of our lists: our personal relationship with God. This is a crucial priority, yet one which most of us are willing to shift to the back burner — or even right off the stove! We may want to be children of God, but we are often reluctant to invest the necessary

4

time in building that relationship. But just as, if you don't talk to your husband or wife, you will soon have no relationship at all, so also if you neglect prayer, Bible reading, and the other elements of communion with God, you will lose that fellowship, as well.

By the way: attending church though necessary, is no substitute for meeting alone with God. Your church will help you develop relationships, and will provide you with opportunities for growth and ministry, but it is not the mediator between you and the Lord! And for the church — whatever church you attend — to help you to grow, also takes time! We must spend time with God, and time with God's people. So many people are "too busy" to pray, or read the Bible, or even think about God.

The Holy Spirit occasionally convicts me in this area. Every now and again I hear His voice saying, "Lorne, where are you?". Even dedicated Christians can get so busy doing good that they neglect their personal relationship with God.

Other Priorities

There are many other time priorities that need to find their proper place in our lives: we need to take time to exercise, to strengthen our bodies; we need time to build relationships with friends and brothers and sisters in the church; we must find time for leisure, perhaps even — it may sound very unspiritual, but — for watching television! I'm not telling you to indiscriminately turn on the tube, but there are certainly, on occasion, programs well worth viewing. I am biased, of course, toward some of Canada's finest Christian broadcasting!

Maintaining a Balance

Our priorities need to find their proper, and consistent, place in our lives. Have you ever known someone who was always finding something new that was vitally important, and temporarily devoting their entire life to it? That is not keeping priorities straight! I have known people who went on such binges — one lady would pray for five hours a day, for a whole month, until someone said, "You really should be witnessing".

5

Well, she would stop praying, and witness constantly, until someone told her she should read the Bible more.

God wants us to have balanced lives.

God's Priorities For Your Time

God has given us principles for setting time priorities. With the guidance of His Word, it is possible to develop a "time budget", just as we should have a budget for our finances. And remember, if you do not devise a plan to organize your time, you won't have any time!

God First!

The reason that I insist that we follow God's priorities for our time is that, if we are to have a healthy and happy life, we must put Him first in everything! I have known a lot of people who have put others before God, and made them first priority — this often happens inside a marriage. But inevitably, a person with skewed priorities like this becomes ill, mentally, physically and/or spiritually. God must be first!

We will be able to adopt God's time priorities as we grow in our loving relationship with Him.

Work

What are God's priorities for our time?

Priority One!

All of these things demand time. There are so many things which demand our time. But God has a priority list. And since He created us, He should know what is most important in our lives! What is at the top of God's priority list for your life?

The answer can be found in Matthew 10:37-39:

"He that loveth father or mother more than me is not worthy of me: and he that loveth son or daughter more than me is not worthy of me. And he that taketh not his cross, and followeth after me, is not worthy of me. He that findeth his life shall lose it: and he that loseth his life for my sake shall find it." (KJV).

6

God First

God must come first. Any personal priority list that does not have your relationship with Jesus Christ at the top is out of whack! And let me stress again: This does not mean that the church comes first. The church's job is to help lead every person into an ongoing personal relationship with Jesus Christ. Many people miss this key to priorities: their wife is more important to them than God is, or their husband is in first place, or their children or their job or even the church. But when that happens, whatever is in first place, becomes your God!

As you read the Bible, you may wonder why "idolatry" is referred to so often. You may think, "Well, that certainly doesn't apply to me in this decade!" But everyone who creates a false God is guilty of idolatry. And any list of priorities that does not place Him at the top, is evidence of idolatry!

Anything in your life that has supplanted God will cause enormous problems. You will lose out on joy and happiness, because our source of eternal happiness can never be people or things — it must be God. So many of the struggles in our relationships are rooted in a false expectation: we expect people to meet needs that only God can meet. Remember, it is God who is able to supply all of our need according to His riches in glory through Christ Jesus.

This basic truth will do much to bring into line our expectations concerning our relationships with people. For example, you do not get married so you can be "happy-ever-after". You don't get married so that your spouse will meet all of your needs. It is unrealistic to expect that when you marry "the right person", all your needs will be met beautifully for the rest of your life. It does not work out this way. Most of us learned this truth in the first week of our marriage!

There is a relationship that will never fail, and that will meet all of your needs, no matter what situation you face, but that is not a human relationship — it is your relationship with God. The Bible is full of stories of people who discovered this truth. The Apostle Paul saw some of his human relationships crumble, but God never failed him, even when Paul was in jail, or being beaten, or shipwrecked, or facing death.

Either you will be in harmony with your Maker and Creator, who is the source of all that you need to be completely fulfilled, or else you will not be fulfilled. It is as simple as that.

Of course, God will use people to meet your needs (just as He will use you to meet their needs), but when they fail you, He will make up the difference. If your spouse lets you down and leaves you for someone else — I trust this will never happen, but if it did — God has promised to be a spouse to you and to fill that gap. That is why He wants you to develop your relationship with Him first, as your number one priority.

According to Matthew 10:37-39, your relationship with God must be more important to you than your own life. If you put yourself first, you have guaranteed disaster! Some people serve God for what they can get out of Him. They say, "God, now I'm going to serve you. You had better bless me!" That's just another way of putting yourself first! Anything that you put ahead of God, anything that you depend on more than you do God, becomes your god! If you do this, it will destroy you. If you depend totally on your husband, the burden will be too heavy for him to bear.

Our Rock in Troubled Times

I have known people who totally fell apart when a son or a daughter died, or a husband or wife passed away. Of course, such a death is always a tragedy. But if God is Number One in our lives, His strength and comfort are there to enable us to grow through such circumstances, to rise in Him to greater heights of faith and fulfilled life. Even after such a loss, God has used these people to bring great blessing to humanity.

I've known people who were in despair because they were not married. They crawl into a little corner, and die. But if God is first in our lives, He will fill these empty spots. Mother Theresa is not married! How much has she given to the world!

God must be first, and if He is in that place in your priorities, He will be the loving source of all that you need.

Give Your Relationships to Jesus!

The best thing that you can do with your other relationships is to give them to God. Give your husband or wife to Jesus.

8

Tell God that this is the most beautiful, precious gift that you have, and that you want Him to have total rights to that person. Tell God that He can take him or her home now, if that is His will. Tell the Lord that your spouse is His. For unless you have that attitude, you will destroy your partner, because you will make him or her a god.

The amazing thing is, when your priorities are straightened out, God will give your spouse back to you, and say, "He or she is mine. Listen to me, and I will teach you how to treat him or her." From then on you are in relationship with the spouse that belongs to the Lord, but who is a special gift to you for you to cherish for the rest of your life. Do you have that attitude?

Jesus said, "As much as you have done it to the least of these, you have done it to me" (Matthew 25:40). When you talk to your wife, it is as though you are talking to Jesus. Be careful how you treat her. It is very important to learn this principle.

Your relationship with God comes first, not your relationship with your husband or wife or children. Jesus repeated this principle in Mark 12:30-33.

"And thou shalt love the Lord thy God with all thy heart, and with all thy soul, and with all thy mind, and with all thy strength: this is the first commandment. And the second is like, namely this, Thou shalt love thy neighbour as thyself. There is none other commandment greater than these. And the scribe said unto him, Well, Master, thou hast said the truth: for there is one God; and there is none other but he: And to love him with all the heart, and with all the understanding, and with all the soul, and with all the strength, and to love his neighbour as himself, is more than all whole burnt offerings and sacrifices" (KJV).

A Commandment Cage?

The scribes and Pharisees had asked Jesus, "What is the most important commandment?" From this passage, we see that God's commandments are not a lot of "don'ts" meant to keep us from being happy. They are not a "commandment cage" intended to prevent you from having any fun. God's commandments are the KEY to your happiness and fulfillment in life. God made these rules because, as the Creator, He knows how He made you. It is something like the situation when a man makes a car. He sends a manual along with it. God's commandments are the manual for fullness of life.

Jesus answered with the most important commandment — "Love God". Everything springs from loving God. Understand this: if you really know who God is and understand how He feels about you, you will love Him. And when you know Him and how He feels about you, you will love yourself. Then you can love your neighbour as yourself. Your closest "neighbour" will be your wife or your husband. True love for your spouse comes no other way. Many people have trouble with their relationships because they do not love themselves. They think that God is angry with them and they really think they are bad. They keep punishing themselves and anybody that gets near them suffers as well, because they can only love in the measure that they can love themselves.

So God's first priority for your time is that before you take time for anything else, take time for personal fellowship with God, all through your life, because it is more important to you and to God than any other demand on your time. If you don't take time for this, nothing else will be right, because everything depends on our personal relationship with God.

Love Those Closest to You

Jesus said that the second most important priority is loving your closest neighbours — the people who are right in your own home. Some Christians make a grave mistake at this point. They believe they are to love God first, and the church second. Many ministers are guilty of putting the church ahead of their families. I know ministers who have chosen their wife solely because that woman will help them in their ministry. She must play the piano. She must be gregarious, relating easily to people. "She must encourage me!" But when they do become married, they are greatly disappointed. And the problem is not with their wife, it is with their priorities!

Family relationships are next in importance to your relationship to God. And in the family relationships, your relationship to your spouse is of primary importance; the children must be secondary. In homes where the children have taken
10

first place in their parents' lives, the result is nothing but disaster. The children become confused, and the husband and wife are alienated one from the other.

Husbands and Wives

The best thing a Dad can do for his kids is to love their mother. That is what produces emotionally sound children. I know women who say, "My children are first, and woe to the man, even if he is my husband, who gets in the way of that. My relationship with my children is first, and everybody better understand that." But that apparently loving action will in reality cause terrible damage to the children.

God has designed the family so that the children must always know that Mom and Dad have a special kind of love for each other. Your children may not yet understand the nature of this love, but it will be a source of great security for them. Never, under any circumstances, should the children come between their parents.

Your family relationships, in the order I have indicated, must come next after your relationship with God. The church comes third. Be careful not to confuse your relationship with the Lord with your relationship with the church. God is first; the church comes later on the list.

Paul, writing to Timothy, had something to say about this question of priorities:

"This is a true saying, If a man desire the office of a bishop, he desireth a good work. A bishop must be blameless, the husband of one wife, vigilant, sober, of good behaviour, given to hospitality, apt to teach; Not given to wine, no striker, not greedy of filthy lucre; but patient, not a brawler, not covetous; One that ruleth well his own house, having his children in subjection with all gravity; (For if a man know not how to rule his own house, how shall he take care of the church of God?)" (I Timothy 3:1-5 KJV).

In this scripture, Paul explains the rules for selection of a bishop or deacon. A man's relationship with his family is a key factor.

11

Some people think that the word "rule" means he is to be an army sergeant, but this is not what is meant, at all. A husband and father is to rule with love. In his home, he is to be an example of loving leadership. There is no suggestion here of the husband acting like a dictator! Instead, he leads by serving. God is calling a man to lay down his life for his family, to serve them, to set the example and to be the responsible one. He is to follow the example of Jesus, who washed His disciples' feet (John 13:3-20).

His home is whole and unified. The same principles that apply in church, apply at home. In fact, the Bible calls the husband and father, "the priest" of the home. Every husband has his own little church — his home. And if a man is not performing that duty well, he will have great trouble if he tries to be a deacon or bishop.

The Word never tells a man to make his wife submit. A man must leave that to God, for a woman will invariably rebel against a man's imposed rule. Instead, if a man follows Christ's example, as outlined for us in Ephesians 5:22-23, all comes right.

Later in that same chapter, Paul wrote: "Even so must their wives be grave, not slanderers, sober, faithful in all things. Let the deacons be the husbands of one wife, ruling their children and their own houses well" (I Timothy 3:11,12 KJV).

Peter wrote: "You husbands must be careful of your wives, being thoughtful of their needs and honouring them as the weaker sex" (I Peter 3:7, Living Bible).

This does not mean that the wife is inferior. It means that she bears children, and that her body is constructed in such a way that she is vulnerable in those times. God instructs men to be understanding, to be supportive for their wives. The passage continues, "Remember that you and your wife are partners in receiving God's blessings. If you don't treat her as you should, your prayers won't get answers." Do you ever wonder why your prayers are not readily answered? You have prayed, but the heavens have seemed like brass. Your problem may lie in the manner in which you are treating your wife. I Timothy 5:8 says, "If any provide not for his own, and especially for those of his own house, he hath denied the faith, and is worse than an infidel" (KJV). Those are strong words. But they clearly show how important the family is to God.

The Church

God's next priority for you is the church. This comes after your relationship to the Lord, and after your family. The fourth priority, following the church, is your vocation.

Our Vocation

We must realize that our vocation comes after our relationship with the church. This is true, even if you are a minister. Many people have their vocation far too high on their list of priorities. This is a dilemma especially for men, and it is one of the major diseases afflicting ministers. They put their vocation ahead of their family, and their children run wild.

We should also realize that in God's eyes, there are no levels of vocation. No job is more important to the Lord than another. After all, it says in God's word that we are all ministers and priests unto God. In Jesus's eyes, a woman at home washing dishes is just as important to Him as an evangelist preaching from a pulpit. To do that wonderful job of being a homemaker — or whatever else you are doing — you will need all of the gifts of the Spirit and everything that God has for you, according to His will. This is the only way you can be a blessing where you are. The truth is, you represent Jesus there. The Lord wants you to do everything as though you were doing it for Him.

It took me a long time to learn that. I used to think, "Lord, I wish that I could get out of this job so that I could be a minister and really do something for you." But Jesus ministered to me, and said, "What do you think you are already doing?" I was in secular television as a producer-director, and I was having quite an influence on the kind of programs that were being produced. God began to show me how great it would be if there was a Christian director-producer in every television station in the country, people who were called by God to be there. And just when I became real happy and comfortable being there, He called me to 100 Huntley Street! If God is our number one priority, He will place us exactly where we are supposed to be, at just the right time.

13

I have encountered so many people who say, "I'm sick and tired of working out there in the world." They think they are working for the devil out there, but they are not. They are working for Jesus. How else is He going to influence society? We need Christian politicians, Christian school board members, Christian teachers, Christian housewives, and Christian garbage collectors. God will never reach our country if Christians all stay huddled together in a little church somewhere, saying, "Oh Lord, the whole world is going to hell", or "It's terrible what the government is doing."

Jesus commended the widow who put her "mite" into the collection box. When we reach heaven, He will have similar praise for women who were faithful to their God-given vocation as housewives and mothers. God is pleased with them. I am not saying that these are the only suitable roles for women, but this role must come second in her priorities, just as being husband and father must be second in a man's priorities, right after his relationship with God. This is the way God has created us. Life does not work any other way. And these roles are far more important than the media suggests: God loves and accepts those people who are hardly noticed in our world.

Love for the Children

Jesus said that the little children would be greatest in His kingdom. He also said, "As much as you have done it unto the least of these little ones you have done it unto me." Moms, when you carried that little baby in your womb for nine months, your job was as precious to Jesus as the job Mary had carrying him in her womb.

I want you to know how our heavenly Father thinks and feels about your children. We see His deep love and concern in the number of times that Jesus referred in love to children, and by the way He blessed them. God says that the value of one person is more than the value of the whole universe. In fact, each individual, man, woman and child, is so valued by God that His Son died for each of us.

This world is in the business of making people feel inferior, and of breeding discontent. The media seeks to make you

14

unhappy with your lot, because these feelings render you vulnerable to their message and their influence. Much of the information that comes at you is directly aimed toward making you feel insecure, unhappy and afraid. Here is a great part of the answer to those who want to know why we have so many nervous problems, inferiority complexes and women suffering from anorexia.

But as Christians, we know the truth: in Christ, we are of enormous worth. Jesus said, "Ye shall know the truth and the truth will make you free" (John 8:32). When you hear the truth it brings peace. The fruits of the Spirit are love, joy, peace, longsuffering, gentleness, meekness. All of these are essential ingredients in stable human beings. And all of these are things we must instill in our children, if they are to be the people God wants them to be.

Children will only learn these things if they see them, as well as hearing about them. Children do not develop as well, emotionally, if they are raised by a single parent or in a home where there is no peace. Our penitentiaries are full of people that come from single parent homes, from homes where there was divorce or who have lost both parents.

Destroying the Family will Destroy Society

When the communists took over Russia, they attempted to do exactly what the secular humanists are doing now in our society. They tried to do away with the family, because they felt they could control the masses better if they could destroy the family structure. In the family structure, people are so committed to one another, and so influenced by one another, that a governmental system cannot break into that natural developmental process. Therefore, such governmental systems will actually attempt to break down the family, to convince everyone that they belong to a larger "Big Brotherhood" family. Thus, the government can gain control. That is secular, humanistic, atheistic teaching.

But in Russia, the separation of children from their parents did not work. They discovered that children need a mother and a father in order to become well-adjusted persons. An increasing number of emotionally disturbed teenagers and adults brought them back to the family unit.

15

The Divorce Epidemic

Who is going to bring us back to the basic family, here in the West? We don't have a state program to divide the family, so we may be less aware of the breakdown. But family breakdown is rampant. We face a crisis. Well over 50 per cent of our children are now being raised by single parents.

Dr. Irwin, a well-known anthropologist, spent his lifetime studying eighty-eight different societies. His findings were that a society which allows the breakdown of family structure is a society which is on the road to extinction. We are a long way down that road. Unless we see a revival of the ability to establish loving homes, we will soon self-destruct, and our place in the world order will be taken by societies which are based on solid, loving homes.

I like to compare the family to a solar system — sun, earth, moon, and the other planets. If they get out of orbit, and one of them is missing, the entire system could disintegrate. God's design for the family system involves a man and a woman, living together for life, and producing and caring for children. If that falls apart, everything around us will fall apart.

Marriage Breakdown and the Economy

Did you know that marriage and family breakdown is one of the biggest negative economic factors in our society? If our homes were stable we would have a more solid economy, because we already have natural resources, and the ability to manufacture goods. We also already have the ability to feed the hungry of the world.

How is our failure to accomplish these things linked to the crisis in our homes? An example of the impact is the housing market. One of the biggest problems in this area is that of couples getting divorced and selling their homes. A man and wife usually buy a house because they want a family; they want to provide a "nest" for their children. But as soon as the marriage breaks up, they sell their house, usually at a loss. Often, bankruptcy immediately follows divorce.

Now, if 50 per cent of all marriages are ending in divorce, what kind of trauma do you think our economic system is suffering?

Add to this slice of the economic crisis, the problem of single mothers living on governmental support. There are many women with small children living at home and being supported by the government, simply because mom and dad could not get along. Do you know that there was a time when, if a man did not stay and work out his problems, remaining faithful to his wife and children, he was considered to be the scum of the earth.

I'm not suggesting we should make everyone feel guilty and worthless, and force them back into ugly situations. Instead, we as a society need to stand with families in crisis, saying, "Listen, you need help. I know that you are having problems, but whatever it is we have got to work together to work this out. Whatever you do, don't run away! You must face this like men and women, because if you do not, it will destroy your children, you, and everything you value."

I am glad that our country genuinely tries to help single mothers. It is good that our government has a sensitivity to this great need. But we should encourage our leaders to be sensitive, as well, to "preventative maintenance", to keeping marriages together so we don't have to support single-mother families in these enormous numbers. We need to begin to train our young men to be good husbands and lovers, and to train our young women to be good wives and lovers.

Our society is trying to help troubled people, but in ways that only promote the problems! There are tremendous tax advantages designed to help single mothers and single fathers, so much so that if they marry, it costs them a lot of money. Therefore, they live in common-law relationships, which further contribute to the break-down of the family! I wrote to the federal cabinet minister responsible for these issues, asking if anything was being done to control benefits going to "singles" who were really in common-law relationships. His reply indicated that there was no way to control that, and besides, the government has no responsibility for the morals of the country.

The Need for Support of Stable Homes

Instead of rewarding family break-down, we should be rewarding those who have established good strong homes!

Through developments such as "no-fault divorce", in which the unfaithful or violent partner is treated equally with the responsible spouse, we have fostered the notion in people's minds that divorce is a way out of problems. It is not! Instead, divorce leads you into worse problems.

The Old Testament only allowed divorce because of the hardness of people's hearts. Of course, if you have a hard heart and continue in that attitude, staying together could lead to something as extreme as murder. But hard hearts are never in God's plan for anyone! The answer is not to split up, but to learn to deal with the problem — to learn to love.

Many people getting divorced today are emotionally crippled because their parents were divorced. Children from divorced homes are twice as likely to get divorced as children from other homes, according to Divorce and the Children, by Vigevenu and Claire.

No Need for Divorce!

This may sound radical, but I want to state it strongly, anyway: There is no reason for you to have to stay together and fight all your life; and there is no reason why you must be divorced! I have seen God perform such beautiful miracles in homes, bringing harmony when there had only been warfare! These were homes where there had been constant strife for five, six, fifteen years, and yet after only a few sessions focusing on God's principles, there was harmony.

A man who beats his wife is usually a man who was raised in a home where his father beat his mother. He hated his father, and is emotionally crippled by it. I advise any woman whose husband is beating her to seek help. Do not let the situation simply continue. But don't give up, either — if he responds to help, God can wonderfully heal that man. I have seen some marvellous examples of such healing.

18

There are some women who, as soon as they are married, immediately turn hurts from their past into attacks on their husbands. They would be husband-beaters if they had the physical strength - and some do! I know one woman who regularly knocked her husband out cold!

In either case — whether a man or a woman is seeking physical and/or emotional dominance — the reason for their behaviour is usually rooted in their childhood. They are like a child, afraid that if they do not have complete control of their spouse, their husband or wife will leave them. They have grown up angry. Even in these extreme cases, divorce is not the answer. It still takes you out of the frying pan and into the fire.

(But let me also state that God is in the business of rescuing people from the fire! So even if you have been divorced, God can meet you where you are, and heal you. Praise God for His mercy!)

Divorce is not — is never — the best answer, despite the message promoted by the media and our government. The government has made it beneficial to separate. Our welfare system and our divorce laws actually encourage someone to desert his or her responsibilities. And with each step, the spiral descends further toward destruction.

We have taught people to be selfish. University sociology courses suggest that marriage no longer works. We are taught that it is unrealistic to expect to have a normal family. Society has "evolved" past that stage. We have entered an age where common-law marriages make more sense, according to the secular humanist experts, and where children should be raised by trained experts. We will avoid child-beating by placing children in specially established nurseries.

We must be concerned with child-beating, of course: it is a terrible thing. But are you aware that children are much more likely to suffer such attacks in single-parent homes? It is directly linked to the same selfish attitudes that produce abortions.

We are being trained in selfishness. According to the dominant, secular humanist philosophy, marriage should not be expected to work. Children should not be a drain on the parents' time and interests, and so it is better if the children be kept

19

in a special facility where parents can spend a few hours of "quality time" with their offspring. None of these things will work: they contravene God's laws and priorities!

Our Need for Family

Within each of us is a need that only our family will fill. If you lack a strong family, you will face severe psychological and emotional problems. Do you wonder why our mental hospitals are full; why suicide rates are climbing; why we are all struggling financially? It is because we have abandoned the "family principle".

I am grateful that finally there is a growing emphasis in the Christian church on families and family living. People are again beginning to learn what it means to be a man or a woman, and how to establish love relationships. It is having an effect. Last year, there were more marriages, and the divorce rate declined slightly. Things have started to go the other way, and I believe this is one sign that we are going to have a revival!

The Bible says that a man's heart will be turned back to his wife and children again. I write this book in the hope that it will be a help to some who need to re-think their priorities.

I thank the Lord for his family plan. I thank Him for making women the way they are, and men the way they are. The devil is attacking God's plan and God's people, but God has said that if we know Him we could have life and have it more abundantly. I pray that you will experience the beginning of abundant life in your relationships, through an understanding of God's word.

Principles
For Healthy Relationships

Demands for Your Time

1) Time for relationship with God!
2) Work: providing for yourselves and your dependents.
3) Sleep: being responsible for your own health.
4) Nutrition: eat right to live right.
5) Relationships: you aren't made to be alone.
6) Exercise.
7) Friendships.
8) Leisure time: take a little TV for relaxation's sake.
9) Extra.

God's Priorities

1) Love God and serve Him (Matthew 10:37-39).
2) Love your family (spouse first, children second) (I Timothy 3:1-5; 5-8; I Peter 3:7).
3) Love the church and serve the brotherhood (Hebrews 10:25).
4) Your vocation (II Thessalonians 3:10-12).
5) All other things follow after these.

The Family

1) Destruction of the family leads to destruction of society.
2) Needless divorce!

To Correct the Dangerous Influences of the Media and Society

1) Husband and wife must spend time together in a special activity one night each week.
2) One night each week must be designated as family night.

For Further Study of the Scriptures from this Chapter

Ecclesiastes 3:1-10	I Timothy 3:1-5
Romans 1:18-32	John 13:3-20
II Thessalonians 3:10	Ephesians 5:22-33
I Corinthians 10:31	I Timothy 3:11-12
Genesis 2:18	I Peter 3:7
Matthew 10:37-39	I Timothy 5:8
Matthew 25:40	John 8:32
Mark 12:30-33	

Chapter Two

Marriage – God's Idea

Marriage is God's idea. There is no need to be afraid of it. One of Satan's greatest triumphs is to make us afraid of the good things that God wants to give to us. We are living in a society that is afraid of marriage. Young men are eager to start a relationship with a young woman, but as soon as it gets "serious", he will pull away because he feels that marriage is very dangerous. This is simply not so.

Marriage is established by God as the Christian principle of support for both a man and a woman. It is the most natural, and the most safe, thing in the world. As a matter of fact, on your own you are very vulnerable. You suffer in sickness much more if you are alone. I once visited a woman in the hospital who could not walk very well. She was in her fifties, unmarried, and all of her family members – mother and father, and sisters – had died. No one had visited her for 10 years! A young single person may not face these traumas, but loneliness can be a deadly affliction in later years. God has planned that our lives should be filled with caring people surrounding us. The most meaningful of these relationships is marriage.

This means, of course, that if someone is genuinely called by God to singleness, they must make sacrifices in order to obey the Lord. For this reason, we should give thanks to God for their obedience, and hold them up fervently in prayer!

Most of Jesus' disciples were married men. This certainly destroys the myth that, if you are really spiritual, really tuned in to God, you don't need marriage. Some, even today, teach that marriage is "copping out" on God's best for you. That simply does not stand up in the light of the scriptures.

On occasion, God does ordain someone to live a single life, but this is the exception to the rule. The basic guideline is laid out in Genesis 2:18: "And the Lord God said, It is not good that the man should be alone; I will make him an help meet for him" (KJV). This occurred in the garden of Eden, before any sin had come into our race. The man was in perfect harmony with God. Nothing stood between Adam and His Creator, and yet, in this beautiful atmosphere, God said that it was not good for man to be alone. This clearly stands against the argument that, if we are close enough to God, we won't need a spouse.

The scripture often used to argue against what I am saying is found in I Corinthians 7. The apostle Paul was talking to a church who was under a great persecution. The Corinthian Christians did not know who would be the next to be stoned to death. In the midst of this situation, they asked Paul about marriage: "Is it wise to marry?"

Paul said this: "Now I will try to answer your other question. What about girls who are not yet married. Should they be permitted to do so? In answer to this question, I have no special command for them from the Lord. But the Lord in His kindness has given me wisdom that can be trusted, and I will be glad to tell you what I think. Here is the problem; we Christians are facing great dangers to our lives at present. In times like these I think it is best for a person to remain unmarried. Of course, if you are already married, don't separate because of this. But if you are not, do not rush into it at this time. If a girl gets married in times like these, it is no sin. However, marriage will bring extra problems that I wish you didn't have to face right now." (I Corinthians 7:25-28 Living Bible).

Paul was advising that it was much better to be single. And I thank God for those people who are single and dedicated to some special part of God's service. God has wonderfully used them and blessed them. But Paul was giving advice for a specific time and circumstance. To avoid additional trauma in a time of persecution, he suggested that it might be good to remain unmarried. But he did not suggest that singleness meant a superior spirituality.

In other passages from Paul's writings, we discover that marriage is the normal state for men and women. For example, let's look at I Corinthians 9:4,5:

"Or don't I have any rights at all? Can't I claim the same privilege the other apostles have of being a guest in your homes? If I had a wife, couldn't I bring her along on these trips just as the other disciples do, and as the Lord's brothers do, and as Peter does?" (Living Bible). One might even deduce from this that the Apostle Paul was wishing he were married! It was only later that celibacy became a humanly-imposed tradition in the church.

The Disciples Were Married

Almost all of the disciples were married men! Does this come as a surprise to you? Only Paul and Barnabas were single. Jesus' brothers were married, and their wives travelled with them in their ministry. By the way, Peter's wife is mentioned three times in the New Testament! The first reference occurs in Matthew 8:14.

The Tradition of Celibacy

A Jesuit priest has explained to me the origins of celibacy for the clergy. The idea of celibacy as a higher spiritual calling for church leaders first came into the Catholic church several hundred years after the resurrection of Jesus. This occurred because the church was overcrowded with priests, and burdened with the problems of the wives and children of priests. Therefore, tight restrictions on the clergy were developed and imposed, including the requirement that priests be celibate.

This solved the problem of the church's responsibility to the wives and children of priests who died. The tradition of unmarried priests and nuns has continued to our day. (However, there are some parts of the world where Catholic priests are married!)

These traditions began to be associated with superior spirituality, but they really were born from expediency, not spiritual dedication. Jesus spoke of these kinds of traditions, and warned us that they must not become a bondage. If God has called you to be single, that is good. As I said, I thank God for the single people who wholeheartedly dedicate themselves to certain ministries — such as Mother Theresa — but it is not to be a bondage.

Matthew 8:14 tells us, "When Jesus arrived at Peter's house, Peter's mother-in-law was in bed with a high fever." (Living Bible); see also Mark 1:30 and Luke 4:38 for the same account). The final reference to Peter's married status is found in I Corinthians 9:5, which we have already considered.

Some Christians, who are arguing that the single state is spiritually preferable, have even suggested that Peter got rid of his wife! That would certainly be contradictory to Paul's instructions in I Corinthians 7. There, just such a situation was taking place: some of the Christians were divorcing their spouses and going into full-time ministry. Paul was their model, and they were erroneously trying to be just like him. Paul's instruction to them was to stay with their wives.

He told Timothy on another occasion: "So I think it is better for these younger widows to marry again and have children and take care of their own homes; then no one will be able to say anything against them." (I Timothy 5:14 Living Bible).

Your Urge To Marriage

You see, every cell in your being pushes you toward the marriage relationship. To deny marriage for yourself is like denying your need for your right arm. You can live without that arm, but it will be much more difficult. Your body, mind, emotions and spirit have all prepared you for the relationship within marriage.

Now, I'm not trying to make single people feel guilty. But I do ask you to be honest with yourself, and to recognize that, deep down inside, you would love to be married. We are designed to share our lives with another in a very intimate way.

To balance this perspective, we also have to admit that there are beautiful opportunities open to single people which married people cannot take advantage of. Therefore, I have to conclude that, whether you are married or single, you can still very much be a whole person, as you walk in the Lord's will. None the less, it is a wonderful privilege to be married.

26

The Cost Of Marriage

This is not to suggest that marriage is "easy street". Marriage will cost you everything. You are called to serve your partner. It is something like being called to the mission field, and it is vital that we remember this. God never wants you to seek after happiness. That's His responsibility, and one He is delighted to fulfill. He'll provide your happiness. The minute you begin to seek after your own happiness, you can be sure you will not find it! Our world is filled with people seeking after their own happiness, and failing at every turn. That is why Jesus said, "He who loses his life will find it" (Matthew 10:39). This is how God has designed us: to serve Him, and to serve others. That's the route to happiness.

You do not marry in order to gain happiness-ever-after. You marry because, in love, you want to serve your partner, and to help to meet his or her needs. Of course, if your partner shares that perspective, you will both find your needs met within that relationship. Here's the key: if you want love, give it away!

One of the major reasons for unhappy marriages is that we so often come into this mission without any training. Again, it's like being a missionary – no one expects someone to go to a foreign land to preach without knowing the language, or to work in medicine without medical training. This is the same problem in many marriages.

"Written In The Stars

When a marriage begins to go sour, many people jump to the conclusion that they must have married the wrong partner. There is a popular modern fairy tale that, somewhere out there, there is your "ideal" partner. It is written "in the stars"! People think that if they can just find Mr. or Miss Right, they are guaranteed life-long happiness. People use the most amazing means to try to find that certain someone: they visit fortune-tellers; they do computer searches for the perfect person. Then they marry, and discover problems that neither the fortune teller nor the computer told them about. They conclude, "I missed it. I got the wrong one."

This same kind of thinking has spilled over into Christian circles, although we have "spiritualized" it. I have heard many people proclaim, "I'm not going to go out and look for a partner. I won't go out with anyone. I'm just going to pray that if God wants me to get married, He will show me." Then they expect to walk out of their home some morning, look at the sky, and see the name of someone written in the sky. The problem with people who function this way, is that they want to walk out the next morning and get a sign to see if God has changed His mind. I also have heard of some fellowships where, if you want to get married, you call together the elders of the church, and tell them that you want to get married. They will pray and tell you whether or not to marry. Really, these people want God to make them into a robot, to make all their decisions for them! But I don't see either of these ideas in the Bible. Instead, I believe that God seldom picks out one person for one person. The Word of God says, a woman "is free to be married to whom she wishes, only in the Lord" (I Corinthians 7:39 NASB).

I believe marriage is something like finding God's will for your vocation. You develop your skills, prepare yourself and then you go out and fill applications, praying that God will guide you. God closes some doors, opens another, you go in and it seems good to you and you begin to apply yourself.

Marriage is similar — you develop friendships, draw close to one, and begin to learn to be one, always keeping your sexuality in line until marriage.

Oh, I know that you have heard stories like: "Even before I met my wife God showed me who she was to be, and then I met her and I knew right away that she was the one." This happens, but it happens very rarely. Most of the time, God leaves the choice up to you, within His principles as shown in the Bible.

A False Excuse

It is both funny and sad that this belief that there is one perfect mate designated by God for you is heard very often from people in troubled marriage relationships. One of the first things they will says is, "Mr. Shepherd, we didn't know what we were doing. We didn't know the Lord, and we didn't ask for His help. We got together for the wrong reasons. That's why we are having trouble. God has told me that the only way we are going to get things straightened out is if I divorce him. We shouldn't be together in the first place." Does that ring any bells?

But the Bible says, "The wife is bound by the law as long as her husband liveth; but if her husband be dead, she is at liberty to be married to whom she will, only in the Lord." (I Corinthians 7:39 KJV). Let's read that again: "She is at liberty to be married to whom she will, only in the Lord." There is no hint of "the perfect, God-ordained person". Instead, she can marry whomever she chooses, as long as it is "in the Lord"; that is, as long as she marries a Christian.

We find another important example in the Old Testament: "And Isaac called Jacob, and blessed him, and charged him, and said unto him, Thou shalt not take a wife of the daughters of Canaan Arise, Go to Padan-aram, to the house of Bethuel thy mother's father; and take thee a wife from thence of the daughters of Laban thy mother's brother". (Genesis 28:1,2 KJV).

Here, again, God says, "Go out and choose". Perhaps the conversation between you and the Lord could go something like this:

"Lord, I would like a wife (or a husband) and I want your will".

The Lord says, "Who would you like?"

You answer, "Lord, I want you to show me the one whom you want me to marry."

And the Lord says, "I want to give you the desires of your heart. Come walk along with me a while, and I will bring a few into your life. Then you can choose."

God loves it when you use what He has given you to make your own decisions. When you use the principles in His word to make your decisions, it will cause you to grow. One of His principles is that you should marry a fellow believer, and thus become one in every sense. Just as when you make love, you are one physically, so when you pray together, you are made one spiritually. It is important that you and your partner have shared priorities, because it is God's idea that your spouse should also be your best friend.

One Step At A Time

Trust God to lead you one step at a time. He is not playing hide and seek with you, and He is not sitting in heaven waiting for you to make a blunder so He can laugh at you. Some people have this picture of God, and they believe that He delights in seeing us blunder as punishment for a lack of commitment to Him. But God isn't like that.

God also isn't a robotics master! Some people would like God to change us into robots. That would take all the pressure off, because then we could turn around (as Adam tried to do) and blame Him if something goes wrong. But God promised exactly the opposite: He said that the truth would make us free! We are the exact opposite of robots — we have been set free in Christ. That is a wonderful truth, but it also means that we have a responsibility for our actions.

People often reply, "Look at Isaac and Rebekah. Didn't God pick her out especially for him? I have always believed that if God picks out someone especially for me, my life will be so much easier and so much happier."

But let's look at this Biblical account of how God helps people make choices. Abraham speaks to his most trusted servant:

"And I will make thee swear by the Lord, the God of heaven, and the God of the earth, that thou shalt not take a wife unto my son of the daughters of the Canaanites, among whom I dwell: but thou shalt go unto my country, and to my kindred, and take a wife unto my son Isaac.

"And the servant said unto him, Peradventure the woman will not be willing to follow me unto this land: must I needs bring thy son again unto the land from whence thou camest?

"And Abraham said unto him, Beware that thou bring not my son thither again. The Lord God of heaven, which took me from my father's house, and from the land of my kindred, and which spake unto me, and that sware unto me, saying, Unto thy seed will I give this land: he shall send his angel before thee, and thou shalt take a wife unto my son from thence. And if the woman will not be willing to follow thee, then thou shalt be clear from this my oath: only bring not my son thither again." (Genesis 24:3-8 KJV).

God desires to give everyone opportunities in life. In this account, He gave the woman the choice. Our lives are made up of a multitude of choices.

In our day, many men are remaining single because they choose not to take the risk of marriage. This is a serious threat to marriage, because it is primarily the role of the man to initiate the marital relationship. A woman has been designed to follow a man who loves her. If a woman takes the initiative in the relationship, it often short-circuits everything in a man and he will pull away, unless he is a little boy looking for a mother.

God Doesn't "Railroad"

In this story in Genesis, the sense of a choice being made is very evident. In Genesis 24:38-41, the servant is speaking, and he makes it very clear that God is not "railroading" anyone — the choice to come or to stay is up to Rebekah.

But thou shalt go unto my father's house, and unto my kindred, and take a wife unto my son. And I said to my master, Peradventure the woman will not follow me. And he said unto me, The Lord, before whom I walk, will send his angel with thee, and prosper thy way; and thou shalt take a wife for my son of my kindred, and of my father's house: Then shalt thou be clear from this my oath, when thou comest to my kindred; and if they give not thee one, thou shalt be clear from my oath."

What is God saying through all of this? From Abraham's words, I conclude that the Lord was telling him something like this: "I am going with you, and I am going to lead you." But there is never any indication that God is going to force Rebekah to return as Isaac's bride.

Remember, God had promised that through Isaac, the children of Abraham would be as the sands of the sea. But there is nothing to indicate that his promise was dependent upon Rebekah. She had her free choice. This is plain in Genesis 24:58.

"And they called Rebekah, and said unto her, Wilt thou go with this man? And she said, I will go." It is important to realize that Rebekah did not receive any sign from the Lord. She had never met Isaac. (God's plan for us usually involves meeting one another and developing friendships, and then, ultimately,

31

making the choice that Rebekah made, sight unseen!). All she knew was that she had been invited to come, and that her father and family were in agreement that she could go. Rebekah took a true step of faith!

However, I am willing to admit that Isaac had more direct guidance from God in the choosing of his wife than some of us should expect. You might say, "I sure would like some of that clear instruction. If the angel of the Lord would point out my spouse like that, so that it is absolutely obvious that this is God's choice for me, I would be happy for the rest of my life. Isaac and Rebekah must have had a wonderful marriage!"

Not A Guarantee

Unfortunately, that is not what the scriptures show us. Here is one example of how Isaac treated the wife God has shown him:

"And Isaac dwelt in Gerar; And the men of that place asked him of his wife; and he said, She is my sister; for he feared to say, she is my wife; lest, said he, the men of the place should kill me for Rebekah; because she was fair to look upon." (Genesis 26:6-7 KJV).

Isaac knew that he was among men who would not hesitate to kill him in order to bring his beautiful wife into their harem. But he did not want to avoid these people because he did good business with them. Therefore, he made this arrangement with Rebekah. What was the result? While Isaac was handling his business arrangements, Rebekah was taken into the harem of another man. Imagine what would have happened, had God not intervened! What a way for a man to treat his wife!

Maybe you think, "My husband treats me just like that". Imagine what Rebekah must have been thinking: "I came all the way from my family and where did I end up? This man is supposed to be responsible for me, and what does he do with me? Here I am, in someone else's harem . . . and all so he can have a successful business deal. He doesn't really care about me. God, what are you doing to me?"

This man Isaac, who was supposed to be a man of God, was completely copping out of his responsibilities to his wife. Even though God had revealed his wife to him in a special way, it didn't help their relationship later on. That's important for us to realize: whatever is in the past, in our marriages, whether good or bad, the important thing is what we are doing now, at this moment, in our relationship with our spouse. ____

Modern-day Isaacs?

Some of you men who are reading this book are guilty of being just like Isaac. You are treating your wives as he treated Rebekah. You are so wrapped up in your own thing that you only use your wife for your own purposes!

This is not the only example of failure in this "marriage made in heaven". You see, it takes more than a God-appointed partner to make a good marriage; it takes work and commitment on the part of both spouses, as they follow God's principles.

Here is another story from the life of Isaac and Rebekah:

"And the Lord said to her, Two nations are in thy womb, and two manner of people shall be separated from thy bowels; and the one people shall be stronger than the other people; and the elder shall serve the younger. And when her days to be delivered were fulfilled, behold, there were twins in her womb. And the first came out red, all over like a hairy garment; and they called his name Esau. And after that came his brother out, and his hand took hold of Esau's heel; and his name was called Jacob: and Isaac was threescore years old when she bare them. And the boys grew: and Esau was a cunning hunter, a man of the field; and Jacob was a plain man, dwelling in tents. And Isaac loved Esau, because he did eat of his venison: but Rebekah loved Jacob." (Genesis 25:23-28 KJV).

How To Ruin Your Children

Isaac and Rebekah could not even agree on the children! They pulled the worst trick ever: each had a favourite child. This attitude guarantees tragedy. As soon as Rebekah favoured Jacob, and Isaac chose Esau as his favourite, they messed up their family, and insured war.

If you do not learn how to walk in harmony and love — a love that plays no favourites — your children will adopt the same attitude of strife, you will have war in your home, and that war will continue through generations, from home to home. There is only one method of teaching children how to love: that is by showing them love.

Rebekah failed in this area:

"And Rebekah spake unto Jacob her son, saying, Behold, I heard thy father speak unto Esau thy brother, saying, Bring me venison, and make me savoury meat, that I may eat, and bless thee before the Lord before my death. Now therefore, my son, obey my voice according to that which I command thee. Go now to the flock, and fetch me from thence two good kids of the goats; and I will make them savoury meat for thy father, such as he loveth: And thou shalt bring it to thy father, that he may eat, and that he may bless thee before his death. And Jacob said to Rebekah his mother, Behold, Esau my brother is a hairy man, and I am a smooth man: My father peradventure will feel me, and I shall seem to him as a deceiver; and I shall bring a curse upon me, and not a blessing. And his mother said unto him, Upon me be thy curse, my son; only obey my voice, and go fetch me them." (Genesis 27:6-13KJV).

Do you see what she was doing? This "ideal wife" for Isaac was conniving and lying to him. She manipulated him and caused his child, her favourite son, to lie and cheat his father. I tell you: when you begin to manipulate the children against one another, all hell on earth is going to break loose in your home.

Learned Deception

A pattern has developed here, a pattern of deceit and manipulation. Have you ever wondered why Jacob was such a liar and a deceiver? He learned it from his mother! And before he ever learned his lesson, his lying ways almost got him killed. Jacob and Esau came to hate each other so much that the two families were ready to kill one another.

Finally Jacob literally took hold of the Lord. He sought God with all his heart, searching for an answer to the problem of enmity between him and his brother. God healed the relationship and changed Jacob, even changing his name to Israel. The fighting stopped from that point on.

This can happen today, too. Sometimes, we think, "This trouble has been going on for years. It's never going to change."

Jacob and Esau finally found peace, after Jacob sought the Lord. Isn't it a wonderful relief to realize that you do not have to fight all of your life?

Our world is now teaching women to manipulate, connive and protect themselves; to do whatever they have to to prevent any man from taking advantage of them. Let me tell you: you cannot protect yourself. Instead, you will cut yourself off from the ability to be in a loving relationship with a man, a relationship that will meet your needs. I often hear women wishing they could end a relationship and start over again with someone else. "If only I could get rid of this guy and start over again. Next time, I really would ask for God's help, and I know God would give me someone who is right for me."

The Bible doesn't say much about finding the right spouse, but it says a whole lot about how to be with your wife or your husband. God's involvement in the choice of Rebekah didn't guarantee happiness later in life. However, if Isaac and Rebekah had followed God's principles, they would not have failed in as many ways as they did.

Hosea's Example

In the book of Hosea we find another example of God giving instruction to a man regarding his choice of a wife. Hosea the prophet had been called to speak a very important message to the people of Isreal. He was to tell them they had committed adultery in their hearts toward the Lord. They had broken God's heart. They had gone after other gods, but God was going to forgive them and to bring them back. To Hosea, God said, "In order for you to know how I feel, and to communicate the message that I have for you, I want you to do something for me":

"The beginning of the word of the Lord by Hosea. And the Lord said to Hosea, Go, take unto thee a wife of whoredoms and children of whoredoms: for the land hath committed great whoredom, departing from the Lord." (Hosea 1:2 KJV).

The Lord told Hosea to marry a prostitute. Aren't you glad God has never given you such a command? By the way, notice from this passage that God does give special direction as to the type of person he wants you to marry. He told Hosea that he wanted him to go out and marry a prostitute. But he never said,

"Hosea, I want you to go down to the corner of Yonge and Gerrard and there will be a girl in a short skirt and black hair, standing there. Her name is Jane. Go up to her and if she repeats a certain sentence after you approach her, she is the one." But this is the kind of direction that Christians are looking for.

No, God wanted Hosea to walk up and down "Yonge Street", and to look around, and find a harlot. The only thing he had to be sure of was that she was, in fact, a harlot. Now, this is a real exception of God's rules. All other instructions in scripture make it very plain that your partner is to be a believer — a Christian — who loves God.

But God is considerate, and allows us to make our own decisions. God told Adam to name the animals; that was his first responsibility. Now, God has told us to find a wife. Let's stop acting as immature babies, and obey God's intentions. God has given us intelligence and the instructions to choose our own mate.

Adam did not say to God, "God, I've got this little thing down here. It's kind of black and it has stripes on its back. It smells, too. What is your will for its name?" If he had, God would have said, "It is my will that you name it. What do you think it should be called?" Isn't it nice that He gives us such choices? But when we misunderstand His guidance, and expect Him to make all the decisions for us, we often miss His will entirely!

How To Put Your Life On Hold

I know a lady, now in her seventies, who believes that God once directed her to marry a particular man. But he married someone else, and she would not enter any other relationship from that time on. There were other men who wanted to marry her, but she would not let it happen. God will not force you to marry if it is against your will. It is up to you to prepare yourself, to be a friendly, loving person. Courtship is based in friendship — keep the sexual aspect of a relationship until you are married. Agree on this with any possible partner, and thus you will not miss God's will in this area.

Back to Hosea, married to a harlot. She left him, and then returned, on several occasions, until he finally, truly learned what God was doing, and then she finally remained with him. In some experiences you need to realize that your partner's weaknesses are good for you.

These two men — Isaac and Hosea — are the Biblical examples used to indicate that God will choose your partner for you. But a close examination of each situation shows that although God gives general direction, a great deal was left to the partners in each situation. And even after this, some of you still feel that you have married the wrong person. You realize that it is possible that, in rebellion against God, you might purposely marry someone, fully aware that you are breaking all God's rules. Perhaps you chose your wife like David chose Bathsheba.

Breaking The Rules

If anyone ever tried hard to break all the rules in selecting a wife, it was David (II Samuel 11,12). He was already married; it is always God's plan for one man to have one wife. Multiple wives is a heathen custom. But David was king, and therefore he thought he could do anything he wanted to do. So he did not bother to ask Bathsheba whether or not she was married. He just brought her over, went to bed with her, and got her pregnant. When he found out she was pregnant he thought, "Oh, man, she's married. What is the kingdom going to think when they find out I've done this?"

So he called her husband, Uriah, home from the battlefield. Uriah was the captain of the army, faithfully fighting for David his king while David was sleeping with his wife! The Bible calls David "a man after God's own heart", but he certainly blundered here, and he suffered for it.

He said to Uriah, "Why don't you take a rest from the battlefield and go home and visit your wife?" But Uriah said, "No I'm a faithful, loyal supporter of my king and when my King is attacked, I want to be in the battlefield, defending him." David's plan to make Uriah think the child was his failed because of Bathsheba's husband's loyalty to David.

When David realized his plan was not working, he sent Uriah back to the front, with a message that guaranteed Uriah's own doom. Uriah gave the sealed message to David's general. It said, "I want you to give orders to this man to run up close to the enemy wall. As he does, the remainder of our soldiers are to fall back and leave him alone so he will be killed." As David had planned, Bathsheba's faithful husband was killed in the battle. David immediately married Bathsheba.

Have you ever tried that hard to go against the will of God? If anyone has tried harder than David to break God's rules, I haven't heard of him.

Then Nathan, a prophet from God, came to David and asked, "My king, a certain man owned a lot of sheep while his neighbour had only one. The man with many went into his neighbour's barnyard, took the one sheep. What do we do with that man?" David said, "Get that man. He should be put to death!" Nathan said, "You are that man."

The prophet warned David that God's judgement was going to come upon him. But notice David's reaction: he immediately prayed. He began to repent, in sackcloth and ashes. Some of the great psalms were written by David in the midst of his repentance. He wrote, "Take not your Holy Spirit from me". He cried, "Don't turn your face away from me," and pleaded with God to "Have mercy on your servant".

After David repented, God did not tell him to separate from Bathsheba! God did not say, "It was never in my plan for you to marry that woman." When God forgives, He accepts us right where we are, at that time, place and circumstance. There is no verse in the Bible which tells you that if you married the wrong one, you should get rid of her or him.

There is one passage which tells us the story of the army of Israel going into a foreign country, marrying the women of that country, and taking them home. God made them return the women. But God said, "They are not your wives — they are wives to someone else in their own land!" The Lord sent the women back to their true husbands. They had committed adultery.

God's Rebuilding Job

God never, ever says, "You married the wrong one, so separate yourself from that one and go and find the right one." If God was going to do that, He would have done so in the case of

Bathsheba. Instead, do you know what God did after David repented? He made that marriage David's best marriage! He had never been close to any woman before. In fact, he said that He had a better love relationship with his friend Jonathan than with any woman. (By the way, the word used there is the Hebrew word for friend; it does not imply any sexual or homosexual relationship. Another word would have been used to denote sexual intimacy.)

No wonder David had so many wives — he did not know how to love any woman. But there is no record in the world indicating that David married any other woman after Bathsheba. He became very close to her. God picked Solomon from that marriage and Joseph who was husband of Mary Mother of Jesus. This is a beautiful example of how God can take a mess and make it right. Remember: no matter how badly you mess up your life, or how much you deliberately rebel against God, God can always make it right. You may think that because you were married out of God's will, you should divorce and remarry or else you will have to suffer for the rest of your life. God doesn't do things like that. I don't care where you are coming from, God can heal your marriage. God's in that business! If God can straighten out David's mess, you can be sure He can handle yours!

My mom and dad were not Christians when they were married, but I know that God approved of their marriage. They came to the Lord when I was about two years old. Actually, Mom had been saved at the age of 16, fell away from the Lord, and while she was backslidden, she met Dad. She returned to the Lord, and then Dad gave his life to Jesus. I know that if they had not come to the Lord, they would not be together today.

Dad had difficulty knowing how to love Mom, because a man learns to love his wife by watching his father love his mother. But my father's mother died when he was young, and he did not have that input. And when Mom was a child, life was difficult because of isolation (they lived out in the country), alcohol and a very unhappy marriage between Grandpa and Grandma. There were constant threats and physical abuse toward each other and the children. Mom had to leave home at the age of 14 because of this abuse. Her younger brother and sister left with her. They travelled over 50 miles to Kingston, Ontario, where they found refuge. Any psychologist would tell you that my mother's life could have been ruined by this environment.

Mom and Dad were right for each other, but if they didn't have the Lord it would have been a mess. But God got hold of their lives, and made beauty from what might have been ashes. It took a number of years for Dad to learn how to love this precious woman, but he did. God had to heal Mom and teach her how to be wife and mother and he did. More than that, my grandmother and grandfather both came to the Lord before they died! My mother watched her brothers and sisters accept the Lord, one by one.

There are many hurting people today, but God can save any of them, and restore any family. That is why Mom and Dad are together today. It took several years for the scars of my Mom from an abused childhood to be healed, but God has done so. And the Lord used my Dad, and their relationship, to speed that healing. They applied Bible principles about love, and then they loved each other. They were committed to each other, no matter what. But while their love was strong, the most important healing love in my mother's life was the love of God.

Aren't you glad that God loves you? If you really love God, you will find that God is always at work in your life. It is important for you to understand this, so that you will not be so afraid of marriage that you avoid it. If you truly want God's will, and you are surrendered to Him, God will bring things together. God has never called you to play it safe. People are wrong when they say, "I can handle my life right now, but if I get married, it's a whole new ball game and I'm not sure I could handle that. So I'm going to play it safe."

Peter was not called to play it safe – instead, Christ called him to walk on water. It's the same with you. If Peter had played it safe he would never have known what it was to be fearful, and what it meant to have his faith grow. The Christian life is an adventure! God wants you to risk everything to trust Him. When we let go of all props and crutches, leaning only on the Lord and not our own wisdom, or security, or circumstances, we are at our healthiest!

I want to give you an example of how God leads. I'm going to show an illustration of how to cooperate with the Spirit of the Lord.

My brother, David, knows what it is to leave your own security, trusting in the Lord. He loved to farm, but he felt called to attend Bible College, and then to enter the ministry. During his first year, I began to wonder if he had made a mistake. He seemed better prepared to be a farmer. As his older brother, I was pleased but very concerned that he wanted to be a preacher.

One man at the college, who was a very able speaker, felt the same way. He told David to face the truth; he did not have the credentials to be a preacher, and he might as well accept reality and head back to the farm. This sounded reasonable, until David remembered that he had felt God's call on his life. One evening, during the time he was really seeking the Lord on this matter, David attended a meeting out in the country. During the service, a young lady gave a message in tongues and then the minister gave the interpretation. The Spirit of the Lord fell with a great anointing. The service was spectacular!

By the way, my brother David is now pastor of one of the leading churches in Ontario and is now in my opinion, an outstanding minister of the Gospel.

David prayed, "Lord, I'm going into the ministry, but please give me a wife like that, who knows the anointing and the tender leading of the Holy Spirit like that woman.

At this time there was a gospel trio called the Clark Sisters. They had ministered in song and in speaking for about five years when they decided to take a year off and attend Bible school to improve their ministry. Some people said, "Oh, you are going to Bible school to find a husband, eh?" Connie Clark was determined to prove them wrong, and she promised herself, "No way. I'm going to show them. We're not going to Bible school to find a husband, and if anybody asks me out, I'll turn them down. I will not take a husband from this college."

Well, David, my brother, noticed Connie. He asked her out for a coffee, and she said no. He gathered up his courage and invited her to have coffee a couple of nights later, and she turned him down again. I guess he decided that she didn't like coffee, so he began to ask her to other things. She said no.

Meanwhile she was thinking, "Who is this guy, David Shepherd? He won't leave me alone. I've got to get him off my back!" Someone suggested that the best answer might be to go out with him once, and explain while they were together that she had no intention of dating anyone. That should discourage him, and David would then leave her alone.

That sounded like a good idea to Connie. The next time David asked, she said yes. Of course, he took her out again and again, and before long they were engaged.

One day my brother and his wife were walking and talking, and he told her of that meeting when the girl had prayed in tongues. He said, "You know, you're exactly what I prayed for. You really know the Lord, you understand the fullness of the Holy Spirit, and your gifts are already alive. God answered my prayer." He talked a lot about God's call on his life for ministry and his prayer regarding his right wife.

She immediately asked, "When was that service, and where?" He told her, and she said, "I was that girl." God not only gave him one like her, but He gave him that particular girl!

God answers prayer.

That's an important principle to remember as you seek to allow the Lord to heal your marriage. If you are having trouble in your marriage, it is not because you once broke God's rules in the past, but because you are doing so now — like Isaac and Rebekah.

If you don't stop breaking rules, you will end up killing one another. You are hardening your heart, but God wants to heal you. The Lord healed David and Bathsheba, and gave them such a strong relationship that David learned, for the first time, how to love a woman! God can do the same for anyone who needs help in their marriage; He brings hope and understanding.

It is important that you have a whole, complete marriage relationship — and not only for your benefit, but for the good of your children. Your children will struggle with the same things that you struggle with. You pass them along, but you can break that pattern by allowing God to heal your marriage. You are able to have a whole marriage no matter what problems you have.

God knows your problems. And there is nothing He cannot heal!

Don't be afraid of marriage. Marriage is God's idea, planned for your own safety. God has ordained every cell of your being for fulfillment that can only happen by establishing a marriage relationship which results in children. God has done that because it is the basis of stability for everything pertaining to our lives.

Principles
For Healthy Relationships

The family is ordained by God. It is His plan of protection for men, women and children.

1) It is usually God's plan for most people to marry.
2) If you don't marry, trust God to help you find other ways to protect you. In the New Testament, the church protected the unmarried.
3) Give yourself to God along with all of your plans for the future.
4) Study and learn how to be a wife or husband and parent.
5) Ask for God's guidance in your choice of a partner.
6) Develop friendships — spiritual relationships with members of the opposite sex, both of you agreeing to keep the sexual intimacies until you are married.
8) If you are now married and you didn't do any of the above, do what King David did: ask God to forgive you and ask him to correct the mess you have made.

For Further Study of the Scriptures from this Chapter:

Genesis 2:18
I Corinthians 7:25-28
I Corinthians 9:4-5
Genesis 24:3-8, 38-41, 58; 25:23-28; 26:6-7; 27:6-13; 28:1-2
Matthew 8:14
Mark 1:30
Luke 4:38

I Corinthians 1:9
Timothy 5:14
I Corinthians 7:39
Hosea 1:2
II Samuel 11,12

Chapter Three

Why We Feel
The Way We Do

Your feelings: what are they? Is what you feel, the real you? Many in our society would say "Yes". Especially in the past 15 years, our society's focus, fostered by the media, has been on feelings. You are warned not to let anyone else tell you how you should feel. You are urged to express what you feel, without much concern for the consequences. You are told you have a right to that expression, and to doing whatever you feel like doing.

According to this school of thought, you are not to allow anyone to inhibit you. You are free to be yourself, to be an individual. Anyone who does not do what they feel like doing is not a whole person!

Let me drop a sobering thought into your mind: Adolph Hitler felt like killing Jews.

God Understands Your Feelings

There is someone who knows exactly what our feelings are all about. In fact, your ability to feel was God's idea in the first place — he put it in you. And He has not left us blind in the dark about the role these feelings are to play in our lives; He has provided us with instructions.

Let's look at the Bible:

"In the beginning was the Word, and the Word was with God, and the Word was God. The same was in the beginning with God. All things were made by him; and without him was not any thing made that was made. In him was life; and the life was the light of men. And the light shineth in the darkness; and the darkness comprehended it not. . . . That was the true Light,

45

which lighteth every man that cometh into the world. He was in the world, and the world was made by him, and the world knew him not." (John 1:1-5, 9-10 KJV).

"And we know that the Son of God is come, and hath given us an understanding, that we may know him that is true, and we are in him that is true, even in his Son Jesus Christ. This is the true God and eternal life." (I John 5:20 KJV).

I thank God that He has not left us blind. He has sent light and understanding in Jesus Christ, and in the word of God. So if we are to understand our feelings, it makes sense to go to the Bible.

"Keep thy heart with all diligence; for out of it are the issues of life." (Proverbs 4:23 KJV). Every time the Bible talks about your "heart", it is referring to that which we call your feelings. We still talk this way, especially in romantic songs about affairs of the heart! But many of those songs suggest that we are swept away, out of control, when our heart is involved. Well, this can happen, but according to this verse from Proverbs, it need not happen! "Keep your heart": did you know that you have control over your emotions? Over and over again the word tells you to watch your heart, for the issues of life flow from it.

"As he thinketh in his heart, so is he." (Proverbs 23:7 KJV). What you think and feel in your heart, is what you become! This is both a powerful, and a frightening principle. It means that you cannot hide wicked or evil thoughts in your heart and enjoy them there, while keeping up a "holy" front. Eventually, you will be what you have been thinking about being.

"There is a way that seemeth right unto a man but the end thereof are the ways of death." (Proverbs 14:12 KJV). What happens if you follow after good feelings? What happens to, "If it feels good, do it?" You enter the ways of death.

"The heart is deceitful above all things and desperately wicked: who can know it?" (Jeremiah 17:9 KJV). Another translation says, "Your heart is terribly untrustworthy. You can't trust your feelings."

These verses throw us into a problem. They tell you to keep your heart with all diligence, and yet warn that the heart will lead you astray and deceive you. If this is true, how are we to

46

control our heart — our feelings? The answer lies in Romans 12:2: "And be not conformed to this world but be ye transformed by the renewing of your mind that you may prove what is the good and acceptable and perfect will of God." (KJV). Paul adds to his instructions to the Romans in Philippians:

"Finally, brethren, whatsoever things are true, whatsoever things are honest, whatsoever things are just, whatsoever things are pure, whatsoever things are lovely, whatsoever things are of good report; if there be any virtue, and if there be any praise, think on these things." (Philippians 4:8). And in the next verse we read, "Those things, which ye have both learned, and received, and heard, and seen in me, do: and the God of peace shall be with you." (Philippians 4:9 KJV).

Media Manipulation

Many of today's experts regarding feelings and emotional reactions work in television. I've been involved in television for 30 years. You cannot be in the medium for that long without learning a great deal about people's feelings and reactions. These things are studied intensely by people in television. They understand your feelings, and are experts at manipulating them.

Much of the input into your unconscious mind was put in when you were a little child. Anything put there at times of fear, anger or sexual shock really sticks! The media uses these things to try to keep the public in a state of fear, anger, sexual stimulation, perversion and disorientation. Television's manipulation is so subtle and efficient that you arrive at certain feelings, believing you have come to that place by yourself. You are unaware of the impact of television on that process. But they have used your unconscious to influence you, and they do it with great skill!

If I asked people if they are influenced by commercials on television, most would answer, "No way! What do you think I am, an idiot? Those stupid things, they make me angry. They never influence me at all!" That reaction is as understandable as it is incorrect. Commercials certainly do influence you. They influence me, and I know what is going on!

You need to understand the impact of the media on your feelings, because many of our problems, especially our inability to develop relationships, come from the media today.

There are several key things that people producing television commercials and programs understand very well. The first is the chain of response: everything which your mind is fed influences your feelings. Your feelings are a mechanism which drives you to act upon that which your mind has been fed. And act on it you will, or the short-circuit in the chain will bring on emotional problems.

Your Unconscious Mind

Let me illustrate this way: Each of us has an unconscious mind. (Some of us live that way all the time! My wife has suggested that is my problem, on several occasions). Your unconscious mind never forgets anything. As a matter of fact, it began to work while you were in your mother's womb. Research has not drawn final conclusions about when this process begins, but they know that by the sixth week after conception, your mind was beginning to react to the emotions of your mother. Researchers have sedated people, and then by activating certain parts of their brain electronically, they have caused those people to recall memories stored in their unconscious mind while they were still in their mothers womb!

Your unconscious mind remembers everything you saw today, whether you consciously noticed it or not. Everything is recorded, and under the right circumstances, it can be played back. Your mind is a fantastic thing! We marvel at the wonders of the computer age, but they have never been able to build a computer to rival the human mind.

Your unconscious mind has recorded everything. You know that this is not true of your conscious mind — we have big gaps in our conscious memory banks. Sometimes I have trouble remembering my name!

Now, of course, much of what you are aware of with your conscious mind affects your feelings. But many of your feelings are reactions rooted in your unconscious, often in memories planted there before the age of six years.

Let me give you an example of how a childhood experience was reflected later in life. My daughter, at the age of 18, was terribly afraid of spiders. I was in the kitchen one day, and she began screaming in terror in her room. I rushed to help, and found a small spider in the corner, and my daughter standing on her bed. This was not the first occurence.

I said, "We've got to do something about this — it's getting worse!" And I asked her, "Were you always afraid of spiders?"

"Yes," said Judy, "Always."

I told her, "No, that's not true. When did it actually start?"

She began to think and then said, "I know when! You were outside working in the garden, and you left us children in the house. We were watching television that Saturday morning. A horror program was on. I was about four years old. There was this great spider, eating people. My sister, who was nine, forced me to watch two feet away from the TV screen. I had nightmares for weeks."

The message put in her mind during that time of terror was, "Spiders eat people."

With the help of the Lord, today Judy is no longer afraid.

In the same way, as you were growing up, the relationships in your family were permanently implanted in your mind. It may have been that your parents fought, or that they loved each other, or that Dad was not around. Whatever the situation, it is implanted in your subconscious. You may remember some of it consciously, but everything is there at the deeper level. As an adult, you react in certain ways and fervently hold certain beliefs, without really knowing why.

The media knows this. They know that the most powerful method of communicating is through a movie. In the movie they have role models: husband and wife, grandpa or grandma, and children. They act out life situations, and you find yourself reacting with feelings that are far more deep than a mere movie should cause. Why? In a sense, the movie or television program bring you into a semi-hypnotic state, and you begin, subconsciously, to become the hero or the heroine. You find yourself crying: a grown adult, crying over a fictional television program! The reason why you are crying is because you are subconsciously identifying with the characters. They are hurt, and you feel it.

Semi-hypnotic State

TV producers know that most people, as they become really interested in the program, enter into a semi-hypnotic state. They revert to being like a little child, easily influenced. Subconsciously, they become the character with whom they identify. If you want to test the intensity of this emotional tie, walk over to the TV while your spouse is watching a program he or she is deeply involved in, and switch the channel. But one warning: this experiment can be very dangerous! The viewer will react as if you have done something against their person! That is how you watch a program: when the heroine is being loved, you feel loved; when the hero is rejected, you feel terribly hurt. A kiss on the screen starts your heart pumping. You almost feel it.

But you are not aware of the intensity of your involvement. You probably say something like, "That was a nice movie", or "I really had fun watching that movie". But the seeds have been planted in your unconscious mind. A day, or a week, or a month later, if you find yourself in a similar circumstance to that of the hero or heroine in the movie, you react as they did. But because it arises from your unconscious, you will not attribute the reaction to the movie; you will believe it came from yourself. If anyone tells you you are behaving like the person in the movie, you will deny it: "No, everyone feels like this!"

It really is very powerful.

Your past experiences plant the same kind of seeds in your unconscious mind, especially traumatic situations. For instance, if when you were a child, there was a lightning storm, lightning hit the house, your mother began to scream and ran and hid in a closet, you may find you are terribly frightened by thunder storms, although you don't know why. You believe that thunder storms are terribly dangerous. As a Christian, you know that you are safe in the arms of Jesus, and you trust him for safety and protection in every circumstance — except in a thunder storm. Then, you run and hide. Our subconscious memories affect us like that.

Animals often behave like human beings. I had a dog, a Labrador Retriever, who must have been traumatized by a thunder storm. I had a lightning rod on my stone house in Kingston, and every time there was a thunder storm, that silly dog would run over to the corner of the house where the lightning rod connection came down. He would lie there and whimper at every roll of thunder. In reality, he was hiding in the most dangerous spot in the house, but you couldn't get him to move.

We often do the same thing. Our fears drive us into the position where we get hit all the time. For example: if your Dad left your Mom when you were a little girl, and your Mom cried, a message was communicated to your young mind that men leave you and you cannot depend on them. If you do not receive healing in that area, when you come into marriage, it will be with a deep-rooted fear that he is going to leave you. Because of that fear, you become over-possessive. You want to know everything he is doing and you are always afraid he is cheating on you. Any time you have an argument, it is a gigantic mountain to you. You over-react, nailing him with everything you can as a kind of advance payment for leaving you.

Small disagreements become mountains, because you expect him to be untrustworthy, and every little problem is more evidence against him. Your thought patterns are confused: "That's right. There he goes again. He's going to leave me. What do I do to keep him? I've got to keep him. I need him. What can I do? I know he's going to leave me. This is terrible!" And these thoughts are probably based only on your subconscious fears, and not at all in reality! If you are not healed in this area, it will be almost impossible for you to trust your husband. You will live a life of constant fear. And fear is not of the Lord!

Patterns Established

Perhaps your mother left your father, or nagged him constantly. This will affect your relationship with your wife. I was counselling a man who, in the midst of an argument, had hit his wife. They were both Christians, and yet he hit her.

He told me, "She was talking to me, and I knew I was going to hit her. I get terribly angry every time she disagrees with me, and I lose control of myself. I can't help it. I can't stand it."

I asked him, "How did your mom and dad get along?"

He said, "My dad was a great guy. He wasn't home very much, though. He was away a lot. But my mom used to nag him and call him all sorts of names. She would criticize everything that he did. She told the neighbours all about it. She would stand out on the street and criticize him in front of the neighbours. I used to get so angry, I would wish that he would just punch her in the nose."

See where it came from? It was programmed in his mind. The message was, "Women nag you". The solution was, "Punch them in the nose".

Of course, his perception was all based in a lie. The real problem was that his father had neglected his mother. He was away all the time and his wife became so lonely that she tried to change him by nagging him. She would criticize him, hoping that if she told him often enough that she was lonely and that she needed him, maybe he would hear, and come to her, and love her. But he just walked away, again, and left her screaming, "You rotten husband!" And the little boy watching that thought, "Boy, I'd love to punch her in the nose once. The only reason he is going is because she is yelling at him."

Jesus can heal a situation like that.

The Serious Side Of The Movies

Let's return to the movies for a moment. Just as real life plants seeds in our unconscious, movies do, as well. That makes the media very dangerous. Many movies and television programs feature unhappy home situations. If you watch this, you will begin to make your partner pay for all the rotten things those terrible men do on television. This is no joke. What do you think watching men mis-use women and women fighting back, does to our unconscious concepts of the relationship between men and women. Do you want to know why we're in trouble?

It is the same mechanism that prompts you to buy soap and deodorant and cologne. We live in a paranoid generation! Everyone is worried that they might have a pimple on their face, or a wrinkle under their eye, or bad breath! One of the primary purposes of television and the other entertainment media is to make you discontented, dissatisfied, afraid, and unhappy with your situation. They know that if you feel this way, you are very vulnerable to their message, and they can control you so much better.

Fear

For example, if they want to sell something to women in menopause, they strike at an area of fear. They will show a woman with gray hair, walking arm in arm with her husband. Suddenly, he is looking over his shoulder at a young girl, and his wife isn't even aware of it. Then the message comes: "Does your husband find you as interesting as he used to?" The intended viewer is already feeling unattractive. She is experiencing the realities of aging. The media know where to hit: exactly where you are already hurting!

She begins to wonder, "Is that what he is doing behind my back?". Of course, that fear did not begin with the commercial — subconsciously, she has been afraid of just that possibility, and the commercial has manipulated her feelings by using her unconscious against her! She decides to dye her hair, and then her husband comes home and asks, "What did you do that for?" Now she is really devastated!

The media does this sort of thing to you, all the time!

Unconscious Programming

Your unconscious programming is so powerful that it would amaze you. It is the source of much of our struggle with our feelings, and the media reinforces the tensions over and over, emphasizing the weakness of human beings, and making us afraid of or angry with one another.

The media knows that you readily accept something if your emotional level is heightened — it really becomes yours.

53

Have you ever, while in the midst of an argument, found yourself defending an idea you really didn't believe at all? But because you were already angry, you claimed it as your own and would have defended it to the death!

This is not news to the media. They have studied you at great length. When they produce commercials, they wire a group of people electronically to test their emotional reactions. They show the program, and then the commercial, and see if the emotional reaction is the one they seek. If not, they make a new commercial. This is the pattern of the major companies who have the money and the expertise to produce the best manipulation.

Do you want to know why our young people are all taking drugs? It started with the Beatles. They made a movie with a couple of songs that glorified the use of drugs and within months the teenagers thought it was cool to take drugs. It has been continuing ever since.

I want you to know that the makers of rock and roll and of a lot of movies are going to stand before God in judgment, because they have massacred more people than Hitler! The media is at the heart of many marriage problems, because they keep emphasizing the negatives.

Dangerous Soaps

Any woman who watches a lot of soap operas — daytime or prime time — will find that she cannot trust any man. And yet no woman will be able to come into a relationship with a man unless she is totally vulnerable and trusting.

On these programs, you watch women being raped and abused over and over again, until finally that woman rises up and beats the man down with a karate chop. God help you, you will be karate chopping your husband about every 20 seconds, in your spirit, even if you do not act it out physically.

The same kind of reactions occur in men. We are programmed every bit as much as women. The media has implanted in us the concept that we are not to love and cherish that woman in deep commitment, but that we are to dominate her and use her. If a relationship gets serious or has any depth to it, you run from her. That's the macho-man image, the Don Juan style. Don't get tied up in a marriage. A real man has all the women at his feet, but no commitment to any of them.

What a pretty picture: men programmed to dominate and women programmed to fight. Jesus wants to stop all that. And He can.

But I Never Faint!

Let me share another illustration of this "feeling" principle. When I was about six years of age, my brother died. He was two years old. I remember a little about the funeral, but not much. Fourteen years later, a friend of mine was killed in a car accident, and I went to the wake. I was in the funeral home for about three minutes and I had to leave, because I was about to faint! As I stood in the fresh air, I was shocked, because I was healthy, 20 years old, and never fainted! So I pulled myself together and headed back into the funeral home. About three minutes later, I started to faint again. I sat down, but that didn't help, and I had to get out.

Sometimes I would be asked to sing at funerals, and I remember that as the worst struggle. Once, at a funeral of a 16-year-old girl who had died in a car accident, the church was full. I was sitting on the platform, and praying: "Lord, help me through this. Don't let me faint. Please don't let me faint." I stood up in the pulpit and I was about to sing when I looked down at the songbook, and it went black. I looked out toward the audience, and I couldn't see anything except black. I hung onto the puplit and I began to sing because I knew the first verse from memory. As I got to the chorus I could see the book again, and I completed the song.

Now, although I thanked the Lord for getting me through that song, I could not understand why I had this problem. Everyone else is sitting there — men, women and even children — and I was the only one fainting!

In my early thirties, as I started to counsel couples, I began to learn about the things from our past which mess up our lives. So I sat down with the Lord, and said, "Lord, when did this happen? Where is this coming from?" Then I remembered the first time it happened: when I had gone to my brother's grave several years after his death. We put some flowers on the grave. I became very faint, and they had to help me back to the car. And I realized what had happend. It was rooted in the trauma of my brother's death. In my unconscious memory were the images of my brother in the casket, and my mother weeping. It caused a fear of death in my heart.

But Jesus says I do not have to fear death. My brother is with Him, and death is a glorious entrance into the kingdom of God! But yet, as a little boy, this fear of death and separation was implanted in my mind. It was such an emotional thing that even as a grown man, I would faint.

Impact Of Divorce

Divorce and broken homes can have a more serious impact than even death! When you come to marriage, these seeds planted in your subconscious can ruin all of your conscious efforts, unless the Lord heals you.

I know of a man who could not stand the fact that his wife sometimes became ill. She would get a little cold and he would become very upset with her and say very cruel things. Just when she needed him, he would become mean and nasty and accuse her of faking her illness.

Finally they went to a counsellor, who discovered that the husband's mother was always ill, and he had constantly waited on her. Whenever he wanted to do something, she would complain and be sick and prevent him from going. He resented this, and his unconscious mind registered the concept, "Women will pretend they are ill and will take advantage of you." When ever his wife became ill, he made her pay for what his mother did. It almost destroyed their marriage.

But Jesus can heal marriages like this.

Your Feelings Are Not You

The bottom line is this: Your feelings are not the real you! Let me stress: Your feelings are not the real you! Your feelings have been programmed into you since you were a child. Your mind retains these things, unconsciously, and your emotions react to them.

After something is programmed into you, it is very difficult to change it. You believe that this is right, and you are ready to die for that concept. For example, if you believe all men are rotten, you become angry if someone says something good about a man. I once noticed a woman in a restaurant. She was trying to get peanuts from a vending machine, but the machine would take her money, and give nothing in return. She hit it again, and said, "Just like a man: it never works!" Then she hit it and pounded it and put a few more coins in, and it produced her peanuts. She said, "Sure; all it needed was a woman".

I've seen the same reactions from men and women. But it is all based in a lie! The best thing in the world for men is women. The best thing in the world for women is men. God created us that way. Men, the best gift God ever gave you, apart from Jesus himself, is your wife. Women, except for Jesus, God's best gift to you is your husband. Believe this, or believe a lie.

Too Dull For Truth

Jesus talked about people who were too dulled to receive the truth:

"In them is fulfilled the prophecy of Isaiah, which saith, By hearing ye shall hear, and shall not understand; and seeing ye shall see, and shall not perceive: For this people's heart is waxed gross, and their ears are dull of hearing, and their eyes they have closed; lest at any time they should see with their eyes, and hear with their ears, and should understand with their heart, and should be converted, and I should heal them. But blessed are your eyes, for they see: and your ears, for they hear." (Matthew 13:14-16 KJV).

The lie is widespread. I talked to one woman who told me she was dating a certain man. I commented that he seemed a serious kind of guy who, when he dates, would be looking for a wife. Normally a woman would react positively to that kind of information! She should be glad that he is sincere, and not only seeking a surface relationship that would lead to hurt. But this woman looked at me with angry eyes: "He wants a wife, eh? Well, if he wants a wife tell him to get a wife. I'm not going to be any man's wife!"

Then I said, "A wife is a beautiful thing!"

Her answer? "I'm not going to be dirt for any man!" She associated being a wife with being dirt! That is what has happened in our society. God referred to this attitude when he said the hearts of men were evil, having "waxed gross". People heard, but they did not hear. The media has taken words we all use, and added negative meaning to them. "Husband" now means "heel"; "wife" often means "nag". We no longer speak in loving and committed tones of our husband or wife.

You have to change your habits! Jesus wants to change your feelings; he wants to change your heart. Jesus said that his sheep hear and recognize His voice. You must begin to listen to His voice, just as his disciples did. You must allow the truth He speaks to replace the lies that have been planted in your unconscious.

Your Will in Action

When you receive any information, you have to decide if it is true or false. If it is false, you must not receive it! Well, a great many television programs are feeding you false information. If you do not reject these lies, and change channels or turn off the set, you will begin to identify with the characters who are selling you the lies! Given a chance to watch a decent program or garbage, you will choose the garbage, because your heart has waxed gross!

I'm going to show you how to change that.

How do you decide what you are going to watch on television? Some people will answer, "by my mood" - I watch what I feel like watching. But there is another, important factor, and it is the key to changing habits.

Have you ever done something you didn't feel like doing, because you thought it was right? What caused that to happen? What causes you to do what is right? The answer is: Your Will. You don't feel like taking the foul tasting medicine, but you swallow it anyway. Why? Your will overrode your feelings. You don't feel like mowing the lawn on such a nice day, but you do, anyway. Why? Your will.

Jesus said that if anyone will, let him come and drink freely of the water of life. He did not invite those to come who felt like coming, but those who came by an act of their will.

58

Our entire society is confused on this issue. We don't know the difference between feelings and will. If you ask someone, "What are you going to do?" they respond by talking about what they feel like doing. Secular humanism has told you to do what you feel like doing. But your WILL decides, not your feelings.

Your will decides what you are going to feed your mind. You are an adult, with freedom of choice. You decide. But remember, your mental diet affects your feelings, and you will act on what you choose to feed your mind. They tell us that if you feed your mind the same thing approximately 36 times, you will act on it.

When someone else attempts to force-feed your mind, we call it propaganda. But whether they try to force you, or you readily receive, the result is the same. Before Adolph Hitler began the genocide against the Jews, he had posters put up all over Germany; posters which depicted Jewish businessmen with little Germans in their teeth. He produced movies showing that Jewish businessmen were a curse on the face of the earth, and therefore should be destroyed. He showed films depicting Jews killing their own babies. This kind of media blitz went on for two or three years, until the German people were ready to stand by and watch the extermination of the Jews.

We are not so different. We readily receive all manner of ungodly propaganda, all kinds of lies. These things have become a part of us. And in doing so, we break God's command: "do not be conformed to this world, but be ye transformed by the renewing of your mind". (Romans 12:2 KJV).

A Tale of Peanut Butter

Do you still doubt the effect of the media on your mind? Here is a silly example - but still true. One Saturday morning, I was relaxing in front of the TV watching, of all things, Sesame Street. Bert and Ernie were on. Ernie had a slice of bread, and announced that he was going to eat it. But after one bite, he said, "This bread is dry". Bert started to get hungry. He began to eat peanut butter, but complained that it was too gooey! Then they decided to cooperate (that was the theme of the piece). The end result, with much discussion of bread and peanut butter, was a shared peanut butter sandwich. Now, jump with me to 3 p.m. that day. I started to feel very hungry. I don't usually eat at 3 in

59

the afternoon, because I stick to very regular meals. I went to the kitchen, opened the cupboard, and saw the peanut butter. Great! I found some bread, and made a peanut butter sandwich. And then I said, "What in the world am I doing. I hate peanut butter sandwiches!"

I've hated them since I was a child, and they were all my Mom could afford to give me for my school lunches. It may have been healthy, but eight straight years of public school peanut butter sandwiches would turn anybody off! And here I was, ready to eat a peanut butter sandwich. TV is a terrible enemy to a balanced diet and normal eating patterns. Television will have you hungry all the time!

The media is terribly powerful!

Because the government recognizes the potential for manipulation, here in Canada there are controls concerning who can appear in certain kinds of advertising. No one can have a role in a children's play and also advertise a commercial product. Celebrities cannot participate in beer commercials.

And yet, because the media's influence is just as strong when the message comes through the program and not the commercials, there is no restriction on the "selling" of drug use, homosexuality, lesbianism, and anti-marriage philosophies. God help us. We need a healing to come right across our nation.

God Knows You

Now, here is the good news. God has a beautiful plan for you, and he cares for you. David celebrated this truth when he sang to God:

"You made all the delicate, inner parts of my body, and knit them together in my mother's womb. Thank you for making me so wonderfully complex! It is amazing to think about. Your workmanship is marvellous - and how well I know it. You were there while I was being formed in utter seclusion. You saw me before I was born and scheduled each day of my life before I began to breathe. Each day was recorded in your Book! How precious it is, Lord, to realize that you are thinking about me constantly." (Psalm 139:13-17, Living Bible).

Again, Romans 12:2 says, "Be not conformed to this world, but be transformed by the renewing of your mind." Jesus said, we must hear his voice and follow his call (John 10:4). Jesus also said, "Come unto to me, all ye that labour and are heavy laden, and I will give you rest. Take my yoke upon you, and learn of me; for I am meek and lowly in heart: and ye shall find rest for your souls. For my yoke is easy, and my burden is light." (Matthew 11:28-30 KJV).

Being Close to God

God is inviting you to get close to Him, because He has already designed the best plan for your life; it is already written down in His book. God made you as a unique creation, unlike anyone else in the world. No one is like you; no one has the same thumbprint as you; likewise, no one has the body, soul, or spirit as you. God made you to be unique, and He has a unique plan for your life! That begins with getting to know Him, as a loving Father.

Many people have a big problem, right here. They identify God with their own father. But their parents rejected them, or hurt them. Perhaps you were abused or abandoned; perhaps you believe you were illegitimate and believe that your parents never wanted you. These things may or may not be true of your own parents, but they are certainly not true of God. He will never abuse, abandon, reject, or refuse us.

I believe there may be illegitimate parents, but there are never illegitimate children. If God waited for perfect parents, there would not be many of us here! He does not reject little children, born out of wedlock. The Bible says that when your mother and your father forsake you, the Lord will lift you up!

Do you think only your parents were involved in your conception? Who do you think gave you your spirit? Jesus was there, involved even in your birth. Parents fail all the time, but Jesus doesn't. He says, "Get close to me, and I'll heal those hurts." I have seen God do some beautiful things for people from very bad backgrounds.

Whatever your hurt, Jesus can heal: wounded relationships, broken marriages; torn lives. Perhaps you have gone through a series of relationships, or of marriages, and nothing has worked out right: Jesus can heal that. You can have the mind of Christ. You can think His thoughts.

Young men receive all kinds of ideas of what it is to be a man, a husband, a father, and a lover. But the only way to truly know what you should be is to be close to the one who made you! Start to believe what God believes about manhood. You will begin to act like Jesus.

The same applies to women. God has designed you to be wives and mothers, but the devil will try to lure you away from those things with his lies. Believing his lies will lead to despair and destruction. But once again, even if those kind of things have occurred, Jesus can heal you, and your relationships.

Programmed for Romance

Both men and women have been building a picture of their ideal mate in their unconscious since they were little children. And then something that seems, on the surface, to be romantically spontaneous, happens. You see someone whose looks, behaviour, personality and ideas all seem to spark something in you. But while it may seem to be romantic and spontaneous, you are actually acting on all of the programing that is part of your unconscious mind. That also helps explain why you might think a certain guy is terrific, while your room-mate can't see anything in him at all!

This may sound terrible, but actually, God made you that way. That means, as long as what has been fed into your mind is right, it is okay! As long as you have a mind nurtured in truth, your emotional responses will be in line.

But did you know that women who are raised by alcoholic fathers usually marry an alcoholic? (See The Transformation of the Inner Man, by John and Paula Sandford.) This happens even though she swears such a man would be the last person on earth for her. Women whose fathers beat their mothers usually marry men who beat them. These things happen because they are following their heart, the heart that the Bible describes as deceitful and desperately wicked. That is why you need to be transformed by the renewing of your mind.

When you come to Jesus, He begins to show you how He feels about you as an individual. He puts His desires in your heart, and you therefore begin to act like Him, and develop His character and habits in your life. When people come to know you they will see rightness and wholeness; they'll sense the very nature of Jesus.

Can you imagine what it would do to your emotional reactions if your unconscious mind is the mind of Christ? You will be joyful no matter what situation you find yourself in. You will be able to deal with it even if you are married to a donkey who kicks you every time you come into the house, if you come in with Christ's love and with wholeness. And you'll be a source of healing to your partner. Wholeness can be very contagious!

Does this help you to understand your feelings? The media is constantly tearing people apart, playing with their emotions, and distorting our natural and right desires for love, and for sexual fulfillment. Believe me, you won't find true love, or sexual fulfillment on a tour boat that looks like a certain boat on television. You'll only find love, joy and wholeness as you draw close to Jesus Christ, and allow Him to renew your mind with the mind of Christ!

You Are Vulnerable!

Let me once more emphasize the impact that the media has on your actions, through your unconsciousness. Many people have trouble accepting the fact that they are as vulnerable to this influence as they truly are. Here is an example of how vulnerable the media believes you are.

In 1985 National Football League Superbowl Game, a one minute commercial cost the sponsor slightly over $1 million. A million bucks for a minute! At half-time, a representative of Apple Computers, who had purchased several commercial spots, was interviewed, and was asked "Is the time worth the price?"

Now, remember: people that buy Apple products pride themselves on skillful decision-making, based on reason. They would deny that they were influenced by televison commercials. Remember, too, that many viewers skip the commercials during a football game, leaving the room, getting a snack, and so forth.

But Apple had also advertised during Superbowl '84. They said that they had once again purchased time because they had very carefully surveyed the sales following the Superbowl on the previous occasion. In the two weeks following the game, they sold $35 million more than in the previous year, and sales continued strong for months!

If a commercial which most people don't want to see, and which aimed at people who skillfully block out ads, can influence them that much, how much more impact will TV have on women who are consistently told to distrust men, and on men who are told, "Don't commit to women; use them; don't have children"?

In the rest of this book, I am going to give you information concerning relationships which is truth. You may react negatively because of the deep-set convictions in your unconscious, but you will be receiving truth. If you will feed your mind these things, and begin to behave the way God planned, you will be free from the lie the devil is communicating through the media.

The media is continually telling people, "You're no good; you're missing out; you're not beautiful; you're too fat." No one can live up to these false images, and therefore, no one likes himself or herself.

Marie Chapian, in her book Love and Be Loved, and Chapian and William Backus, in Telling Yourself the Truth, argue that the media has drained each of us of self-esteem. And no one can build a loving relationship with anyone else unless they see themselves as a lovable person — unless you see yourself as God sees you. God knows that you are beautiful, and He loves you more than the whole universe!

You are a creation of great value. This is not said from pride, but as truth. You are as valuable as anyone else, for God loves us all!

You must escape the negative media trap. If you have problems loving yourself, do this: write down a list of all your faults, and ask God to forgive each one. Then tell God you forgive yourself. Turn the problem of any changing that needs to be done in you, over to God. You can't bring about the proper changes, because you don't even know the type of person you should be — only God does!

Don't wish you were someone else. Thank God for you!

Now, make a second list, of your good qualities. Keeping going until you reach ten. Read that list morning and night, and thank Jesus for each one. When a new good quality occurs to you, add it to the list. Do this for 36 days. You'll begin to see yourself as God sees you and you will have cast down evil imaginations (II Corinthians 10:5).

Principles
For Healthy Relationships

Let me stress: because of inculcated habits, some of what is said in the rest of this book may bring the reaction: "No way!" But remember the process of "programming" that has already been performed upon your unconscious by the media.

Unconscious Mind

Conscious Mind

Feelings

Actions/Behaviour

What the Media Knows: How Habits are Formed

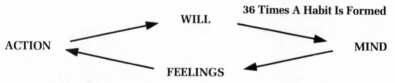

36 Times A Habit Is Formed

WILL

ACTION

MIND

FEELINGS

How you feel is not the real you. Your feelings are only a sum total of what your mind has been fed!

For Further Reading:

I have found the following books to be very helpful in the areas discussed in this chapter. For further reading regarding our inner feelings, read: Transformation of the Inner Man, and Restoring the Christian Family, both by John and Paula Sandford. For an excellent summary of the impact of secular humanism on and through the media, see The Battle for the Mind and The Battle for the Family, both by Tim LaHaye. and for an excellent study of the kind of situation I personally encountered regarding my fainting spells at funerals, see Healing For Damaged Emotions by David Seiman.

For Further Study of the Scriptures from this Chapter:

John 1:1-5, 9-10
I John 5:20
Proverbs 4:23; 23:7, 14:12
Jeremiah 17:9
Romans 12:2

Philippians 4:8-9
Matthew 13:14-16
Psalm 139:13-17
Matthew 11:28-30
II Corinthians 10:5

Chapter Four

How To Love

In the English language there is only one word for love; simply, "love". But in the Hebrew and Greek languages there are several words, all of which we translate as "love". These different words have very different meanings.

For example, in Greek, the language of our New Testament, "fileo" is used for friendship love; "agape" indicates God's love or spiritual union between people of like spirit; and "eros" is used to refer to the physical, sexual intimacy between a husband and a wife. By the way, did you realize that God created your sexuality? The devil certainly didn't do it. And when God completed His creation — including two sexual beings, male and female — He said, "It is good".

You Need Three Kinds of Love

In your love relationship you need all three types of love. There is yet another type of Biblical love: the love that a mother has for her child.

Our English language falls short in this area: we have only one word that we generally use to mean all of these things — the word "love". Hollywood has a field day with this word, and with the confusion caused by all of its many meanings. When Hollywood says "love" it almost always means "erotic passion". But this isn't what the Bible primarily refers to, when it refers to love relationships between a man and a woman.

Marry Your Best Friend

Of course, if you love there will be feelings of passion, but God's first intention is that you marry your best friend. If you are going to share the rest of your life with someone, it might as well be your best friend!

It is also in God's plan that you be one, spiritually, with your partner. It is His goal that you will share your innermost feelings, the things that are the most precious to you. As you share this way with each other, you will walk together as one. You must share an experience with God and a love for Him. It is obvious that your spouse should be a person with whom you can pray, and with whom you can be comfortable in that spiritual sharing. As God answers your prayers, your partner should be the first one you share praise to God with.

Marry a Spiritual Partner

Far more important than passion is shared devotion. A good marriage is one in which you walk side by side with a partner with whom you are spiritually one.

Some people are only married to friends, but not to spiritual partners. They never pray together. They never talk about God or about the eternal questions that occur to all of us. They never talk about dying. God wants you to be married to a friend, but to more than a friend — to someone with whom you can share concerning these deepest questions and concerns.

And when you are friends, and are spiritually one, the other part of your love relationship will truly come to life! "Fileo" love and "agape" love make "eros" love — or passion — all the more wonderful! As I noted earlier, God created sex, and sexual desire. It is His desire that you have erotic love. He wants you to be in a relationship in which you can share your most intimate self, for the rest of your life. This is what the sex act is meant to be. It is not only a physical act; it involves sharing your complete, intimate self.

Sexuality: At the Heart of a Person

Your sexuality is never only physical. It is at the heart of your whole person. Everything you are is very much either male of female. Many of the reasons that lie behind your actions center on your sexuality.

It is God's intention, then, that you walk through life with someone toward whom you have a lifetime commitment. You need to be bonded together sexually, meeting one another's needs for the rest of your life. That is not ony fulfilling, it is also a guard against misdirecting your sexuality. In such committed relationships, there is true pleasure. We live in a generation where sex is the most common topic of conversation. But although everyone talks about it, most people continue to be frustrated in this area. This is simply because they have left out the main ingredients necessary to fulfilled sexuality. The only time sex is genuinely fulfilling is when you share a life-time commitment with your best friend with whom you are spiritually one!

"Knowing"

That relationship allows sexual fulfillment in an atmosphere of trust, faithfulness and mutual understanding, or "knowing". It is not an accident that the Bible refers to sexual intercourse as "knowing" your wife or husband. That simply reflects God's overall plan for intimate sharing on all of these levels. You truly will "know" one another, intimately.

Love is Doing!

To understand God's principles for love, we also need to realize that love, in Biblical terms, is never "feeling", first of all; it is always "doing", always "an act of the will". God is not telling you to feel anything; He is telling you to do!

This intimate relationship with a partner with whom you share fileo, agape, and eros love, will never just happem — you have to do something. None of these things exist on their own, and the entire relationship of love is impossible if we do not develop it, in commitment to our partner, by an act of our will.

In the Hollywood version of love, this sense of personal responsibility is entirely missing. In their stories, someone is zapped by Cupid; all of a sudden you're in love. It just happened that way! and then, five years later, the husband comes home and says, "Honey, I don't love you anymore. I'm sorry, but what is a guy going to do? That is the way love is. It is nice while it lasts, but it goes away, and that's the way things happen. I find myself in love with a girl at the office, and if I stayed with you now, I would be acting like a hypocrite. It would be hard for you."

Commanded to Love

Let me tell you: I am glad love is not like that! God has never suggested that love is a self-sustaining feeling; instead, God commands us to love, as an act of our will. Emotional highs may fluctuate, but that has absolutely nothing to do with real, godly love!

In Ephesians 5:25, Paul made this very clear: "Husbands, love your wives, even as Christ also loved the church, and gave himself for it." (KJV). Paul isn't discussing feelings — he is telling husbands to do something.

You might be interested to know that in Paul's day, the husband had little to say in the choice of a wife for him. There was often a family arrangement, and the husband and wife were "stuck" with each other. And yet, even in that sort of circumstance, Paul talks about a husband's responsibility to love his wife. You see, Hollywood romance has little or nothing to do with love. Husbands are to love wives, now, even if they did not "fall in love" with them first!

This may seem radical, but nowhere in the Bible does it say, "Be sure you are in love before you get married." "Being in love" refers to that emotional reaction, one to another. And this is nowhere near the most important aspect of Biblical love. We do not have to "fall in love", but we are commanded to "love".

I'm not speaking against romantic, emotional attachment. That has been created in you by God, as a push toward a marriage relationship. This is very strong. Your idea of an ideal partner has been fed into your mind, and has been forming there, since you were a child. But while we are prompted by our emotions, we only act on them by a choice of the will. We have already seen that God wants to direct us toward proper choices as we allow the Spirit to renew our minds.

I believe that God's ideal is for a man and a woman to choose each other as partners for life. But the scriptures plainly teach that if a marriage is arranged some other way, love is still a command.

In the same chapter of Ephesians, Paul wrote, "So ought men to love their wives as their own bodies. He that loveth his wife, loveth himself." (Ephesians 5:28 KJV). Remember: if God tells you to do something, He will make it possible for you to do it! He tells us to love our partners as much as we love our own bodies.

Acting in Love

I have encountered many wives and husbands who say, "How can I love that person? Can't you see how terrible he (or she) is?" You can love that person, but only as you act in love The media is constantly encouraging us to act in anger. That will only lead to destruction. The Bible says, "Husbands, love your wives, and be not bitter against them" (Colossians 3:19 KJV). You see, you are faced with a choice between the two. You can love your partner, or you can be bitter. But not both.

Over and over again, the Bible tells husbands to love their wives. But only once does the word instruct wives to love their husbands! ("That they may teach the young women to be sober, to love their husbands, to love their children." [Titus 2:4]). Do you know why? This is because women will usually love someone who loves them. God has made women in such a way that they will respond to a man's love.

Many men have grabbed onto the verses about "submission", and they go around like army sergeants, demanding of their wife: "You submit to me!" God did not create women to submit in circumstances like that. It is no wonder there is much female rebellion today! God created women so that their submission comes as a normal response to a man's love for them!

Love God? Love Your Spouse!

John wrote, "If a man say, I love God, and hateth his brother, he is a liar: for he that loveth not his brother whom he hath seen, how can he love God whom he hath not seen?" (I John 4:20 KJV). This is a strong warning. And it especially applies to marriage, because the closest brother or sister you have is your husband or wife! If you do not love your spouse, God says you do not love Him!

You might say, "Well, you don't know the rotten guy that I live with". No, but God does, and He loves him anyway! God never tells you to do anything you can't do. If He says, "love", you can love!

71

What does God mean when He tells you to love? He answers that question best for us in I Corinthians 13. Even a little child can understand the instructions in this beautiful and simple passage. And notice: nowhere in the chapter does it tell you to "feel" anything. It says, "do this"! Perhaps you are thinking, "Oh, but I want those feelings!" Well, that is the wonderful thing: the surest way to have those feelings is to do what God tells you. Then, the emotional reactions come, too!

I Corinthians 13:4, in the Living Bible, is translated, "Love is very patient". God is telling you to love by being patient.

Jealousy is not Love

We are also told, love is "never jealous". The Bible says that jealousy is as cruel as the grave. Some people are very mistaken about this. I've heard a woman say, "See how jealous he is? He must love me very much". But many a jealous husband has killed his wife! That is certainly not love. Jealousy arises from a selfish motivation, from the feeling that "I'm not getting what I want out of this". Therefore they decide that they are going to have their partner — to own their partner! — "and she (or he) had better pay attention to me all the time, or I'll kill her!" Does that sound like love? That is only possessiveness, which smothers you. It is destructive for both people involved.

True love is "never jealous, never boastful or proud, never haughty or selfish or rude. Love does not demand its own way. It is not irritable or touchy. It does not hold grudges and will hardly even notice when others do it wrong. It is never glad about injustice, but rejoices whenever truth wins out. If you love someone you will be loyal to him, no matter what the cost. You will always believe in him, always expect the best of him, and always stand your ground defending him. All the special gifts and powers from God will some day come to an end, but love goes on forever." (I Corinthians 13:4-8, Living Bible).

Constant Forgiveness

Let me suggest that it can all be stated like this: God is telling you to keep your partner in a state of constant forgiveness. Forgive him or her just as God forgives you. Give all our rights over to God. Stop trying to protect your rights. Do not judge your partner, because you are not equipped to judge. Only God knows what kind of partner you need. He knows what your needs are before you ask! He has said that He is able to supply all of your needs through Christ Jesus.

It is God's plan to supply some of those needs through your partner. But if your partner fails in those areas, God will make it up to you. He is always the ultimate source of every good gift! Because this is true, there is no person on earth nor demon in hell that will be able to take one thing away from you that God wants you to have, if you have given all of your rights over to Him!

This is why Jesus said that the first commandment is to love God with all your being. That is where we are safe. People in our society are afraid, because they do not trust in God. They are afraid as they choose a partner, so they choose ever so carefully, trying to meet their *own* needs, and then the partner lets them down! It doesn't matter who you marry; at some point, your spouse will let you down. They will fail you, and you will fail them! If you are leaning totally on them you will fall when they do. But if your trust is first of all in God, and if you are experiencing and offering the forgiveness of Christ, you will not suffer harm. You may have to take some strong action, but if you do it with a heart of love and forgiveness, it will bring healing to you and to your partner at the same time.

People in our society are so busy trying to protect themselves that everyone is tearing everyone else to pieces! Jesus is telling you that He will protect you; trust Him to meet your needs! In the Sermon on the Mount, He said, "Blessed are ye, when men shall revile you, and persecute you, and shall say all manner of evil against you falsely, for my sake. Rejoice and be exceeding glad: for great is your reward in heaven." (Matthew 5:11,12 KJV).

No matter what you may suffer at the hands of your partner — false accusations, dirty tricks, persecution — God will reward you for your loving faithfulness, over and over again, in this life and in the life to come. Even if your spouse went insane and murdered you tomorrow, you would enter heaven and the greatest blessing you have ever known. As the apostle Paul said, "Sudden death, sudden glory". Understand if your partner is trying to kill you stop him but do it with love, not with anger and hatred.

Family Persecution Predicted

Jesus said that in this world, His followers would have tribulation, so it should not come as a surprise. He also said that much of this persecution would come through family members. It will happen to you, but it will not harm you if you forgive.

God wants you to surrender all of your rights, and your hopes and dreams and plans to Him. It is not that He wants to take these things from you. In fact, it is God's will that you have abundant life, happiness, and all that is good. But the Bible says that unless a grain of wheat falls into the ground and dies, it abides alone. But if it does fall into the ground and die, it will spring forth and bring up fruit. That's what you must do with your rights, hopes, dreams, and plans. Give them up to God, and then you will see what He will produce from that seed.

You see, you are not getting married to have all of your needs met. You have given them to God, and He is already meeting your needs. Your responsibility, in your marriage relationship, is to love and bless your partner, and, eventually, your children. If this is not your intention, you will never be happy in your relationship.

I realize that this idea is directly opposite to what we are taught by the modern media, but it is true, none the less.

Unconditional Love

Your love must be unconditional. If your love has conditions attached, neither your needs nor those of your partner will be met, because there is never a time when you need love more than when you have failed. Only unconditional love that is there in the bad times is true love. Love that you have to earn will never meet your real needs. And love that your partner has to earn because of your imposed conditions will never meet his or her needs. Therefore, I say: give up your rights and concentrate on keeping your partner in a constant state of forgiveness.

Let your commitment rest in your love, not in their actions. Let your partner realize that your love is unconditional, and that he or she can depend on you, with no strings attached. Even if they fail you, and stop loving you, your commitment will remain firm.

Right now you are thinking, "That's almost suicidal!" No, it is not. If you have that attitude, people will not tend to take advantage of you; instead, they will love you. The Bible says that "Others will treat you as you treat them". (Matthew 7:2, Living Bible). If you want love, give it away.

God is telling you to decide that you are only going to think loving thoughts about your partner. When he or she makes mistakes, you are going to forgive, and trust God to change him or her. Your partner's sins are actually none of your business. They are really a matter between them and Jesus. They may hurt you, but the sin hurts the Lord most of all. So we can trust Jesus to deal with these things.

He said that He was going away, but that He would send the Holy Spirit. The Spirit will "reprove the world of sin, and of righteousness, and of judgement." (John 16:8 KJV). That is not your job; it is the responsibility of the Holy Spirit. Your job is to love one another as Christ loves the church. How did Jesus show His love for the church? He bore all our sin, and said, "Father, forgive them, for they don't know what they are doing", and when we come to Him and confess our sins He forgives us. And He says that this is the type of love that He wants, between a husband and a wife.

You might say, "That makes me totally vulnerable". Right! And if one partner in a marriage is willing to be as vulnerable as Christ is to us, a beautiful healing will begin in that relationship. Think loving thoughts, say loving words, commit loving acts, and leave the changing of your partner to God. God has not programmed your partner to respond to your attempts to change them. You don't know what changes are truly necessary anyway — only the Holy Spirit sees the heart.

Leave the Changes With God

And as surely as He sees your partners heart — and yours! — He knows what changes need to be made, and He will begin to work in your lives. God is committed to you, and will meet your needs. But if you try to do it yourself, you will only make a mess of everything! If you continually emphasize your partner's faults, you will only guarantee that those areas will become worse.

75

We get a sense of who we are from the reactions of those closest to us. If we are continually reminded of certain faults, they will become exaggerated in us! You can be devastated if everything you hear about yourself is negative, and nothing is positive. You will begin to believe that this is the whole truth about you!

Let's think about the example of a football player. The team is about to take to the field for a big game. One thing the coach would never do, is remind a player of all of his faults and weaknesses. That would only guarantee that the player would fail. The coach seeks to build up and support the players so they will be at their best in the game.

The same principle is true in marriage. Yet I have known so many couples who continually remind one another of failings and weaknesses. They have their lists and they will not let go! No wonder they fail when the pressure is on. God will have to work twice as long to bring about any change in a person whose spouse is continually pointing out weaknesses and failings!

In our day, we have become very skilled at criticism. We justify it: "Listen, somebody has to straighten him out, and it might as well be me". But Jesus had something to say about this: "Judge not, that ye be not judged. For with what judgment ye judge, ye shall be judged: and with what measure ye mete, it shall be measured to you again". (Matthew 7:1 KJV). People are not programmed by God to receive criticism from other people. There is a barrier in you, placed there by God, that rises up to block such criticism. Instead, you have been created to respond to the gentle, loving Holy Spirit and to God's love.

Have you ever tried to be a friend to someone who was constantly telling you all your faults? You pull away immediately. Well, if you are always pointing out your wife's faults to her, don't be surprised if your friendship disappears!

If you have ever stood as the accused in court, I'm sure you did not fall in love with the judge! But in our homes, we set ourselves up as judge, or accuser, and then are surprised when your partner does not react in love! God has made us to love, not to accuse. By His gentle Holy Spirit, He will bring about the changes. It is not our job! Only God knows what is right. If we start to judge, we are actually setting ourselves up in God's place!

76

Judgment is Contagious

What happens when you judge? The person whom you are judging returns the favour. With the measure that you mete, you will be measured! Criticism breeds criticism, and it will destroy the home. Many television shows which feature families entertain us with constant criticism. It may be funny to hear, but it will produce hell in the home. Women are taught to criticize, to "put their husbands in their place". That will devastate the man, and destroy the home. Men are taught to do the same, and the woman then becomes vulnerable to some other man who will speak words of love, instead of criticism. And it destroys the home.

The solution is to compliment one another, cherish one another, communicate to each other they are special.

If every couple reacted to one another in criticism when they first meet, there would be no couples! What brought you together was the positive feedback you received from one another. He said, "You have beautiful hair". She said, "I like your sweater". And so on. What would have happened if it had been this way: He says, "You have an ugly nose"; she says, "You really sounded stupid in class today." What are the chances for that relationship? If it wouldn't work when you first met, why do you think criticism is OK now? No loving relationship can begin on the basis of criticism, and criticism will destory a love relationship already begun. You began by speaking loving words and thinking loving thoughts. That's the right pattern to continue.

Constant criticism creates an additional problem: you begin to have a critical spirit, and you cannot look at anyone without criticizing. I have known people who are so used to looking for faults that nothing will satisfy them anymore. They can't stand anything about their partner. If it continues, the marriage will break up, or the critic will have a nervous breakdown, because if you feed yourself negative thoughts, which produce negative emotions, this will prompt you to act. If you don't act, you will fall apart.

A sad pattern can be established. The critical partner goes to a secular marriage counsellor, who says, "Obviously, you are not happy, so perhaps you should leave." You leave, and find relief, because you have taken action to alleviate your own emotional pressure. You have convinced yourself that your partner was a dirty rotten heel, the worst person on the face of the earth. "How could anybody live with him?" You then find another partner, become married again, and the entire pattern starts again. The problem isn't the partner, it is your criticism, and you leave a trail of devastated people in your wake.

It is not God's will that this kind of inter-personal activity take place in your home. You may have long-standing patterns established; in fact, if you were raised in a home where they fought all the time, the pattern of criticism is already programmed into you. But the Lord wants to — and will — change this into His habit pattern.

Intercession

The Bible says that Jesus is standing before the throne in heaven making intercession for us, day and night. Sometimes I imagine it like this:

Jesus says to the Father, "You know that boy of mine down there, Lord? He is a really good guy."

But Satan is also standing there, and he says, "But God, look what he did! I've got a list right here!"

Jesus says, "It's all right. I'm teaching him. I convicted him and he almost listened to me last time."

But Satan answers, "But he's not going to listen. I know him. He's a stubborn so-and-so."

Jesus says, "Yes, he's a little bit stubborn, but he has responded at times."

Now, which side do you stand on? Which side does your attitude line up with? Are you with Jesus, standing before the Father, making intercession and emphasizing the positive things, or are you standing with the accuser?

Jesus has promised that if you confess your sins, He is faithful and just to forgive your sins and to cleanse you from all unrighteousness. But I've noticed that we much prefer to confess faults than sins, and even more so, we prefer to confess someone else's faults! If I were to sit down with you, right now, and ask you to tell me something good about your partner, you might have to think for a while. But if I were to ask you to tell me one of your partner's faults, I suspect you'd have a hard time stopping at one!

I rejoice that Jesus has left us complete operating instructions for this complicated thing called life. One of the important things He said was: "And why do you look at the speck that is in your brother's eye, but do not notice the log that is in your own eye? Or how can you say to your brother, 'Let me take the speck out of your eye', and behold, the log is in your own eye? You hypocrite, first take the log out of your own eye, and then you will see clearly to take the speck out of your brother's eye." (Matthew 7:3-5 NASB).

These instructions are very clear.

Confession

James wrote, "Confess your faults one to another and pray for one another that you may be healed." (James 5:16 KJV). What gets healed? Among other things, the faults do! By the way, those faults are usually caused because you are believing lies. Whenever we are believing lies, we are crippled. The Lord calls on us to confess them. This applies in the church, but also in the family, in the closest brother-sister relationship you have — with your spouse.

Confess your faults one to another. This is the road to healing in a marriage relationship. And these "faults" do not have to be things that seem enormously important on moral or spiritual grounds. For example:

A husband (call him "Joe") always leaves his boots in the middle of the floor, because he was raised on a farm and his family wasn't too fussy about such things. But this really irritates his wife, Jane, because she is a city girl, and things were always neat in her home. Joe knows this, but every once in a while he forgets, and Jane finds those boots in the middle of the floor. This is a fault, because it irritates Joe's wife, and he knows it. Now, what will happen if Joe comes to Jane and says "Honey, I'm sorry. I've left my boots in the middle of the floor again, and I know better, but I fail you sometimes, and I'm sorry".

How will Jane respond? Most probably, she will be reminded that she has faults, as well, and she will forgive Joe, realizing that he is human too.

The truth is, honest confession seems to prompt honest confession! The marriage will become much stronger, because Joe and Jane will adopt the custom of confessing faults. What you are really saying is, "I need your understanding." You are allowing yourself to be vulnerable with your spouse. And you are saying, "I trust you enough to let you know where I fail and to understand the failure and to forgive me. I need your understanding and I need your help."

A woman will climb over fences to find a man like that!

Forgiveness: The Cure For Hurt

We have to be vulnerable to one another, to let down the defenses. You have built those defenses on the foundation of past failures — you've been hurt, and you don't want to be hurt again.

But the only cure for hurts — past and present — is forgiveness. Relationships can never recover from hurt unless there is forgiveness. Perhaps you hate your father, or you cannot love your husband. The only answer is to forgive! You cannot defend yourself from being hurt — you'll only be hurt in another way.

The apostle Paul said, "I die daily so that I help the brethren of the church" (I Corinthians 15:31). God has not called you to defend yourself, to seek your own happiness, or to make your mark on this world. He has designed you to be like Him — to concentrate on blessing everyone who comes near you! A mother has no trouble being a mother if she decides to be poured out for her children. It costs a mother everything to be a mother, because she lays her life on the line. This is how a mother can give great love to a retarded child, for as she pours herself out for this child, seeking to be a blessing to him or her, she will not resent the inconvenience of the situation.

This is one of God's great laws of human relationships: if you do nothing but live for other people all your life, you will be the happiest person on earth. I haven't seen a man or woman yet whose needs have not been met when they have lived a poured-out life. It really works.

You might ask me, "What if you live in a very abusive situation?" You sometimes have to take some very serious action in an abusive situation. But even then, the one who decides to act in love will be the happy one.

Acting in Love

Let me share an example: A man and wife who were on the verge of divorce came to me. They hated one another; I knew that as soon as I heard them talk. When they sat across from one another, they glared! But within weeks, they were transformed and loving one another because of this principle.

Another couple came to me for counselling. The wife had telephoned: "My husband and I are having trouble with our marriage. My husband is really very unhappy and I don't know why. Can we make an appointment with you?"

During the session I ask her, "Are you happy with marriage?"

"Oh yes, I'm happy," she said.

I asked her, "What do you think of your husband?"

She answered, "He's a good man."

I asked her, "Any complaints?"

She answered, "Not really."

So I turned to the husband, and I said, "You're not very happy. What is wrong?"

He said, "I just don't have any feelings for her anymore, I'm unhappy with life and everything turns out wrong for me. I think it would just be better if I got away from the married situation. If I were single, maybe I would find myself out there."

As we talked, I discovered that he had a habit of losing his temper from time to time. He had slapped her around several times. I asked the wife if that was true. "Oh yes, but you've got to understand that he had a bad childhood. I've been praying for him, and he hasn't slapped me too much lately."

I asked him what happens on those occasions. He answered, "I don't really know. Things bother me, and then . . .".

I asked, "How is your sexual relationship?"

He answered, "Not really very good. I tried a few affairs with other women but that wasn't any better."

I said to the lady, "Did you know that he was running around?"

She said, "Oh yes, I knew that he went out with a couple of other women, but you've got to understand, he's going through a struggle right now."

I asked her how she felt about that, and she said, "It really hurt me but I forgave him, and I think I understand, now. When the Lord heals him from the struggle he'll be OK. And that's why we're here."

She was calm Her nerves were fine. She was happy. In the natural, she had every reason to hate that bum. But if she had, she would have been a wreck. Instead, she turned her spirit loose to God to meet her needs. In the middle of that storm she had peace.

I ministered to her husband, and took him back to his childhood. I found that he had lived through a horrible situation in his home. His father was a very immoral man, and his son had learned the same patterns. We applied inner healing and some counsel in that area, and he is a happily married man now. Together, they are serving God. God healed their marriage and made it whole.

Principles
For Healthy Relationships

Here is what God is telling you to do, when He tells you to love (I Corinthians 13:4-8):

1) Give up all of your rights, to God.
2) Hold your partner in a state of constant forgiveness.
3) Leave the changing of your partner to God.
4) Spend the rest of your life planning ways to bless your partner.
5) By an act of your will,
   a) Think loving thoughts
   b) Say loving words
   c) Commit loving acts.
6) Confess your faults and failures to your partner (Matthew 7:1-5; James 5:16).
7) Put aside time regularly for communication in an effort to understand the other person.

For Further Study of the Scriptures from this Chapter:

Ephesians 5:25-28
Colossians 3:19
Titus 2:4
I John 4:20
I Corinthians 13

Matthew 5:11,12
Matthew 7:1-5
James 5:16
I Corinthians 15:31

Chapter Five

How To Put
Love Into Action

There is nothing more misunderstood in our society than this thing called "love". Our world has a hundred definitions for love, and almost all of them are wrong.

In a previous chapter, we read I Corinthians 13, the "love chapter". Here is something we did not read there: "Love is something that you feel very strongly and if you have that feeling then you will do all sorts of loving things." But although you will never read that in the Bible, almost everyone believes it!

Here is something else not found in the Bible: "Love is blind". This is simply not true. Love is not blind, and that makes unconditional love all the more marvellous, because love is then based in forgiveness, not in ignorance!

Love forgives. You do not try to change your partner; instead, you choose almost not to notice when they do wrong. This is unconditional love: loving your partner in spite of their actions. This is God's principle for loving. God is telling you to keep your partner in a state of constant forgiveness, to be vulnerable to your partner. And then God tells you to choose, by an act of your will, to think loving thoughts, to say loving words and to do loving actions. Leave the changing of your partner up to God, because you can't do it anyway.

The Negative Impact of Trying to Change Your Partner

As a matter of fact, if you try to change your partner, it will produce the opposite result. Your partner will get a mental image of himself or herself by what his closest love tells him about himself. If you constantly point out to your partner all the

85

areas in which he or she fails you, your partner will get a mental image of himself as a failure. Remember, whatever you feed your mind, your feelings push you to act upon. Feeding criticism to your spouse will create behaviour patterns exactly opposite to what you want to accomplish. So give it up!

You need to understand that if God doesn't give it to you, then you are not going to get it, no matter how much hard work you do. God wants to give you a full life. He wants to give you love. Therefore, you must give up your ambition to get love for yourself. Until you let go, God will stand back and wait for your invitation to let Him do what He wants to do for you. He wants you to trust Him to give you all the love that you need. He will bring much of that love through other people, but you have to release your desires to Him before that can happen.

In our society, we have been taught another way. We have been told to protect ourselves, to fight for our rightful place, to allow no one to get in the way. You can follow that model, but you will never find love, a full life, or the peace of God.

The Cost of Loving

It will cost you everything to love. That's a big price, but it is worth it, because it will cost you even more if you do not love! If you don't love, you will die emotionally, physically and spiritually. This is what Jesus was talking about when He said, "Unless a grain of wheat falls into the earth and dies, it remains by itself alone; but if it dies it bears much fruit." (John 12:24 NAS).

Paul wrote, "Put on therefore, as the elect of God, holy and beloved, bowels of mercy, kindness, humbleness of mind, meekness, longsuffering; Forbearing one another, and forgiving one another, if any man have a quarrel against any: even as Christ forgave you, so also do ye. And above all these things put on charity." (Colossians 3:12-14 KJV). The Living Bible says to "put on love".

Back in the days of King James, when the scriptures were translated, they knew more about what love is. Love is being poured out, giving whether you feel like it or not. That is what a mother does when she gives birth to a child. She puts her life on the line.

This scripture says, "above all these things put on charity, which is the bond of perfectness. And let the peace of God rule in your hearts." (Colossians 3:14-15). Then, the peace comes.

On one occasion, recorded in John 13, Jesus' disciples were arguing over who would be the greatest in the Kingdom of Heaven. Jesus brought in a towel and a basin of water, got down on His knees, and began to wash their feet. He was illustrating that great principle: he who would be the greatest of all, let him be servant of all.

Love and Service

We have mixed it all up, in our society. We think that those who are in authority are the important ones, but they're not! In God's mind, the servant is most important. If you want to do something special for God, be a servant. That is the only way to happiness. Only those in authority who also have a servant's heart are good rulers. Otherwise, they act like dictators. Everyone will hate them, and they will thus cause crippling in all of those who are under them.

After washing their feet, Jesus told His disciples, "The servant is not greater than his lord; neither is he that is sent greater than he that sent him. If ye know these things, happy are ye if ye do them." (John 13:16,17 KJV).

The last phrase is important: not only are we to know these things, but we are to do them. A lot of us know them, but fail to put them into practice. Sometimes that is because it is very difficult to change a habit. We are afraid because that is what will kill you! Habits are interesting things. No matter how evil or dangerous a habit is, it becomes a comfortable part of you, and therefore feels right. You become secure in your pigpen.

Leaving the Pigpen

In deciding to read these first five chapters, you have chosen to feed your mind some important information with regard to loving. That is the first step toward changing your habits. You have begun to open the door so you can leave the pigpen! In an earlier chapter, you learned about the link between what you feed your mind, the impact on your emotions, and the emotional push to act on it. This is how you got into bad habits; this is how your habits will be changed! As you realize these new truths concerning love, you will begin to feel comfortable with them.

What you are facing is the need to start something new in your life, something that will bring wholeness and the ability to love. You will develop the ability to have a friendship-love relationship. You will also have the ability to allow "agape" love to flow, bringing spiritual union that will do wonders in the area of sexual intimacy! Following God's principles will transform all of the aspects of your love relationship.

Maybe you're thinking, "This is just exactly what I've been looking for!" Then, read on! Or maybe you're saying, "This sounds too good to be true. Besides, Lorne, you don't know the kind of donkey I'm married to. You don't know the hell on earth he has made of our marriage!" Let me encourage you, too, to read on. God's principles are for everyone, in every situation. He can make that donkey into a deer!

Give God Your Burden

It is God's plan that you, by an act of your own choosing, think loving thoughts, say loving words and commit loving acts. It is God's plan that you hold your partner in a state of constant forgiveness, trusting God to change him or her. You can change no one. Only God can. So it is important for you to put down that particular burden. You were never meant to carry it.

List the Faults

Here is how you start: get alone somewhere, and write down a list of all your partner's faults. Write down all of those things that you have grieved over and wanted to see changed. It may be a long list. I remember one young woman who got to sixty-five things on the list, and was still going strong. And she had only been married two years!

She had come to me with her husband, and halfway through our first session she erupted: "I've had it with him. This is his last opportunity! I'm bringing him in this time and if this doesn't change him, I'm finished!"

I knew right away who had the problem. I asked them to each write out one of these lists, and she filled pages! I knew he wasn't all that bad: he was a good worker, and a Christian. He provided well for the home, and never beat her up or called her names. But when the wife was young, her dad had left home and her mom had several nervous breakdowns because of it. She used to stay with her grandmother. Her grandmother hated her grandfather. This young wife had been prepared, all through her life, to ruin a marriage. She was suspicious of men and very self-protective. So I asked her to write the list.

You do the same. And when you have finished, go back to the top and have a talk with the Lord. Start at number one, and say, "Jesus, I forgive him or her for that fault, and I ask you to forgive him or her. From now on, Jesus, the problem is yours."

The Bible teaches that with the mouth confession is made unto salvation. It is important for you to speak these things. You have to take some action. "From now on, I have decided to let go. I had a whole lot of ideas of what I need in a partner, Lord, and I tried to bring that about, but it's not working. So I turn that changing over to you."

Go down that list and talk to the Lord about every one of those things until you get to the bottom. Now, don't you dare show your partner that list, because most of the stuff on it is garbage. There are exaggerations and distortions. You have set yourself up to be a judge, but only God is able to judge.

When you have finished bringing all of those things before the Lord, and you have stated your forgiveness in each area, and given them to Him, I want you to burn that list. Isn't that what the Lord does when He forgives you? The Bible says that He removes it from us, never to remember it again. I'm so glad that He doesn't fling my sin in my face again.

You need to realize that you have been guilty of judging. Ask God to forgive you for judging your partner. Don't tell God that you are sorry about the way that you feel, BUT it really was your partner's fault. Don't make excuses. Do ask God to forgive you.

List Good Qualities

After you burn that list, make out another list. Write down all of your partner's good qualities, those things that you appreciate about him or her. Let me warn you: if you have been in the habit of concentrating on the negatives, you may not be able to think of many. But you need to change your habit patterns. Keep writing the list of good qualities until you have ten. Yes, there are ten! Ask the Holy Spirit to help you.

Our friend with 65 faults could not think of any good qualities when it came to this list. Together, we began to find a few good things: he didn't beat her; he provided for her. But this principle worked in her life. A week after she wrote her list of good qualities, the number of faults she was aware of in her husband were down to three. From over 65, down to three! After three weeks, she said that those three didn't matter any more. Now, that couple is wonderfully happy, and have a new baby!

Thanksgiving

After you have listed ten good qualities, I want you to take that list and review it every morning and night, and thank God for those good qualities. Praise God for them. Did you know that the Lord dwells in the midst of the praises of His people? When you begin to thank God, the Holy Spirit will come right into the middle of your relationship to bring love and to teach love to both of you. He comes in an attitude of thanksgiving. It is His desire to straighten out your lives, but He will only work when you give the problem over to Him.

Anything good in your partner comes from God, for every good gift is from Him!

Did you know that if it was not for God, your partner would have killed you long ago? That sounds crazy, but it is true, because there is murder in the heart of every man. It is only the grace of God that prevents this. Have you been thanking God for this kind of protection? God has been protecting you all along. You don't have to protect your rights, because God has sent His angels to protect you, and Jesus is making intercession on your behalf before the Father. All heaven is available to protect you, if you will accept it.

As you go down that list each morning, thank God for each thing on it, and add anything new that occurs to you. In doing this, you are "being transformed in the renewing of your mind". (Romans 12:1,2 KJV). In the past, you have gotten out of bed each morning remembering all the faults of your partner. Now,

90

you have begun to feed your mind a different diet, from God's menu. With the help of the Lord, you will begin each day differently, thanking God for the good things in your partner. After you do this for about 36 days, you probably won't need the list any more.

But remember, if you dwell on the negatives it won't be long before they seem as big as mountains. You won't be able to stand anything about your partner — the way he talks, the way she breathes, the way he walks. I knew a woman who had fed such negative things into her own mind that when her husband walked into the room, she ran to the washroom and vomited! Your feelings will push you to act upon whatever you feed your mind.

"I Love You"

Here's another thing that will make a great difference in your relationship: at least once a day, tell your partner that you love him or her. Say to your wife or to your husband, "I love you." You may react to this suggestion by saying, "That is no good unless I feel it. I don't want to be a hypocrite. Besides, she'll be able to tell that I just said it, without feeling it."

But do you know that there is power in spoken words? And are you aware of what you are saying when you say, "I love you"? You are not saying that you have wonderful, fantastic feelings about her so that you can hardly control yourself and you cannot keep your hands off her. That may be Hollywood's picture of love, but it isn't true. When you say "I love you", you are simply saying, "You can depend on me. If everybody else fails you I'll be there even if it kills me. I am committed to you."

This is what God says to me, every day. His love doesn't depend on some emotional whim. God says, "Lorne, I would die for you again if it was necessary.". This is the first thing He tells me when I am disobedient to Him.

In the same way, even when your partner fails you they need to hear that you're not going to desert them. And isn't that what you need, as well? So when you say, "I love you", you are just restating your vows. "I am committed to you. Whatever happens, I'll be here. Even if you go insane, I'll be here."

91

I remember the story of an evangelist, who for the first time planned to have a healing line as part of the service. They had prayed about this, and believed it was God's will for them to minister healing to people at the meeting. The first woman in line was a lady with demonic problems. She began to scream and spit at the evangelist. She fell to the floor and began to writhe like a snake and bark like a dog, and do all sorts of other things the Bible speaks about. Eventually that evangelist, with some other men, prayed for her and she was wonderfully delivered.

That evangelist said that this lady's husband stood there, beside her on the platform, through the entire situation. He stood with her as she writhed and cursed and spat. God spoke to me through this. He said, "Lorne, look at that husband. Nobody would have blamed him if he had committed that woman to an institution, divorced her, and found another wife." But instead he stood in public commitment to her, even at her worst moments. Imagine the home life in that family, the problems and the hurt. But he stood with her.

The lady became a very healthy, normal woman. The family is a healthy, normal family, and God has blessed them. God will reward that husband because he was committed to his partner. That is love.

Tell your partner at least once a day that you love them. And attach to that statement one of their good qualities: "I love you and I really appreciate the way you . . .". Remember that your partner will become what their loved ones tell them they are!

Bad Actions, Not Bad People

This is why, when you are raising children, you should never call them "bad boy" or "bad girl". They will begin to see themselves that way. I have talked to a little boy and said to him, "You're a good little boy". He said, "No, I'm a bad boy". I later discovered that his father always told him that he was a bad boy. It would be far better to say, instead, "You're a good boy; why are you doing all these bad things? Good little boys don't do these bad things." He gets his mental picture of who he is by what his mom and his dad tell him he is. He feels, and then begins to believe, that he is a bad boy. Then he thinks, "Well, I'm a bad boy. I guess I'd better do bad things."

The priciple is the same with adults. And that is why your partner needs to hear, coming from your mouth, those good gifts and blessings which God has given to them. I do not mean phony or dishonest things. You don't say, "Honey, you have the most gorgeous hair in the world"; but you can say, "Honey, I really appreciate and love the way you keep your hair."

At least once a day, tell your partner, "I love you", and add to it one of their good qualities. I want you to know that there will be at least one new additon to that list each day. It may be a one-time thing, such as, "I like the way that you reacted to the neighbour when he really got angry at you. You did not get angry in return. That was really good." Even if it happens only once, tell your partner about it.

Experts at Insult

In our society, largely because of the influence of the media, we are so skilled at pointing out faults to one another. You can walk onto any school ground and watch them tear one another apart. If any child has a deformity or a speech impediment, or is different in any way at all, they can be torn to pieces!

By the time we reach adult-hood, we are so trained in negative patterns that we are ready to give our partner a shot before he or she can give us one. We must stop that habit. And when you get used to telling your partner that you love them, and praise them for their good qualities, you will have solved the bad habit. You will be constantly encouraging and expressing a thankful heart to your partner.

Men as Leaders

It is important for men to take the lead in this. The Bible tells men, over and over again, to be the leader in the love relationship. We have a society of men who don't know how to love women at all. We're like that foolish man who said, "I told you that I loved you on our wedding day, and when I change my mind I'll let you know." She needs to hear your profession of love every day. A woman gains much of her self esteem from what her husband tells her about herself. She needs to hear that you love her and appreciate her.

She will even test you sometimes. If you say, "I really love you," she'll say, "Why?". You answer, "You have so many special qualities". She'll say, "What are they?" The best thing you can do is to give her a loving answer that shows your appreciation for the good things about her.

Positive Praise

We've talked about thanking God for the good things about your partner; and expressing appreciation to your partner for these things. Now, let's go beyond that: at least once a week, when you are in the presence of friends or especially of relatives, allow yourself to say, "I really love this person. Do you know what she (or he) does?" And then tell them all about one of the good things that your partner does, or the good characteristics she or he has.

You may feel slightly foolish the first time that you do it. You know that the "in" thing today, when couples get together, is to cut one another up. "Take my wife for instance. Please, somebody, take her!" You may laugh about it, and she will come back with another remark, like "Who would take him?" This is very bad humour, and it leads into serious insults and offenses.

When you are out in company, stand against this kind of negativism. Instead, tell them, in your partner's presence, that you really love your partner. And tell them some of the reasons why.

Using Inlaws as Storm Troopers

Do you know why so many people have serious problems with their inlaws? It is because when you fail in an attempt to change your partner, and you are grieving about it, you give mom a call at home and you dump all of your complaints on her. Subconsciously you hope that the next time mom sees your spouse she will really let him or her know all of his or her faults, and maybe your partner will change.

Use your head! This is not going to work! Mom begins to think that she has to save her son or daughter by changing their spouse, so she awaits her opportunity. Everybody comes home for Thanksgiving dinner, and the family is sitting around the dining room table. That's when Mom brings up the delicate subject and hopes that the whole group will gang up on him or her and make the person feel really guilty so he or she will change.

But all you have really accomplished is the alienation of your spouse from your relatives. Your husband or wife will never want to see them again.

You have no busines doing this. It causes enormous trouble, and won't solve anything. Instead, let your relatives and your friends know that you love and cherish this person.

Loving Actions

Now let's move beyond words to actions. Once a week, commit a loving act. Do something that you know really pleases your partner. Ask God to guide you in this. Do something that you know he or she likes, and make it something different every week. Buying roses once is great; buying roses every week quickly becomes just another habit. Do something different that your partner will like.

The important thing is for you to get started in these new patterns. You must be transformed by the renewing of your mind. The only alternative is to live in misery for the rest of your life! That is the sure result if you try to change your part-ner: it will destroy your relationship. The only successful way is God's way! He is dedicated to protecting your rights and to giving you everything that He has planned for you. He has planned good for you; He has planned that you should be loved. When you apply these principles, you release God to go to work.

Let me suggest one other thing that will improve your re-lationship. Once you begin to use the principles I have already suggested, start another new habit: for fifteen minutes every day, sit down, put your arms around one another and talk to-gether.

We live in a society where the television or the radio is always on, or where you are continually running here and there. As you run past your spouse, you kiss-on-the-run, and keep going out the door. One of the most frequent complaints from women is, "He never talks to me. He comes home at night and he says, 'What's for supper'. He sits down and eats supper, and then he plunks himself down in front of the TV. If I ask him what happened at the office, he says, 'I worked'. If I ask him what he is doing tomorrow, he says, 'I'm going to work'. then he goes to bed and mumbles 'Goodnight'. He gets up in the morning, says 'Good morning', reads the paper over breakfast, and leaves for work."

Do you see the problem? We are leaving no time in our lives for communication with the person that should be closer to us than any other human being! Let me assure you: if you get this love principle working, you will want to talk, but if you continue in criticism and judgement, no one will be talking!

So every night, for 15 minutes, talk to one another. Talk about the things that are important to you. Talk about your problems; about things you have never expressed to anyone. Talk about your expectations. Remember: it is not your job to force your expectations upon your partner, but you can share with them how you feel about things. Do not blame them for your feelings; they're not responsible anyway! Do you understand that? Your partner cannot force you to be angry; you choose to get angry! Your partner cannot make you unhappy; you choose to be unhappy. The key to your emotional health is how you choose to react to the circumstances which you encounter. You can get angry, or unhappy, bitter — or you can release your rights to the Lord! Isn't it wonderful that you can have happiness in the middle of the most extraordinary circumstances?

Let me give you an example of how this can work out. I'm the villain of this particular story!

Not long ago, my wife had an operation which removed a bunion from her foot. After the operation, her foot was put in a cast. She could get around pretty well, but it was awkward, and somewhat painful. After a day's work, her foot was swollen and more painful.

One day, after she finished work, she came to my office (we work in adjacent buildings) and said, "Honey, I think I'll go home. I'll take the car."

I glanced up and said, "O.K., here are the keys". Just then I was paged by our receptionist who said, "There is someone here who needs to see you right away. It's kind of an emergency".

I gave my wife a peck on the cheek, said "Goodbye, honey", and she left. I then concentrated on the visitor with the problem. But about 20 minutes later, I was paged again. I picked up the phone and heard my wife's voice, asking, "Where's the car?"

I have some faults. A big one is that I occasionally get so busy ministering to others that I forget my wife. I suddenly realized what had happened.

Normally we park our car in a parking lot, but that day the parking lot was filled, and I parked in another place. I forgot to tell her. She had hobbled all the way to the parking lot with the cast on her foot, searched for the car, and finally came all the way back to ask me what was going on.

Now, I should have left my visitor, gone and brought the car to the front door, and helped her to the car. But I was still too busy with other people! That is a dumb mistake which we men make all the time. Instead, I told her where the car was, and she hobbled off to drive home. I went back to my counselling session.

It was fairly late when I got home that evening, but my wife was still up. She said, "Hi, Honey, do you want a cup of coffee or a bite to eat?" So we sat down for a coffee together. She asked me about my activities that day, and we talked about my work. And then, just as we were getting ready to go to bed, she said, "Do you know, honey, that when I got to that parking lot and didn't find the car, I was really angry."

Do you hear what she was saying? She was not blaming me for her anger. She was confessing her own feelings. For a moment she was very angry with this husband!

She did not meet me at the door with a tirade: "You neglected me! Everyone else is more important to you than I am!

Why don't you practice what you preach?" That would probably have ended with her handing me a pillow and a blanket, and an invitation to sleep on the couch!

Instead, she served me a coffee, talked with me, and then confessed her own anger. She did not judge me. She knew that it might be that the young man needed me at that very moment. She trusted God to deal with me in those areas.

Usually, I am a pretty good husband. But I slip up. If you were to ask her what kind of husband I am, she would tell you I'm one of the best! I have listened to her brag about me.

Do you get the point? She confessed her anger, and that honest, non-judgmental communication opened the door for my confession of my much greater error. She did not accuse me, but I instantly responded, "Honey, I'm so sorry. I blew it, didn't I? I neglected you, and I put someone else first, again. You are a very special woman. I should have gone and brought the car to you."

She said, "It's all right. I know that you are helping people."

I said, "But I should have cared for you first. How is your foot?"

Do you see what her wise confession produced? Our communication brought us even closer together. An accusation would have driven a wedge between us. This is a vitally important principle for every married couple!

If you can sit and talk about how you feel without the interference of trying to change one another, that atmosphere of love will produce a communication ability which will transform your marriage. But you need to practice this principle. You need to talk for at least 15 minutes each day, probably in the evening.

You may be reading this, and you are on the brink of a divorce. I believe, on the strength of the word of God, that if you begin to put these principles into practice, your marriage will be completely changed.

1) First, make that list of your partner's faults, express your forgiveness for each one, and give them to the Lord;

2) Second, list your partner's good qualities and begin to thank the Lord for them daily, adding to the list as new qualities are apparent; keep going until you have ten.

3) Third, begin to tell your partner that you love them, and that you appreciate their good qualities; and name at least one per day.

4) Set aside at least 15 minutes each day for honest, but non-judgmental, communication.

What will happen? Everything good! Changes will take place in your heart, and then in your partner. It will be so easy for your partner to be close to you, because it is always easy to be near someone who is constantly encouraging you and pointing out your good qualities. Love will blossom.

Principles
For Healthy Relationships

1) Face the unloving habit as a sin. There is never an excuse for sin — you are always responsible for your own sinful behaviour. You can never rightly blame someone else — no one can make you do anything!
2) Confess it as a sin, that it is hurting God and hurting everyone who gets close to you.
3) Ask God to forgive you (I John 1:9).
4) Ask God to fill you with the Holy Spirit, so that He will give you God's ability to love (Romans 5:5).
5) Thank God for doing this.
6) Repeat the above process every time you fail in this area.

Remember Our Old Habit Diagram!

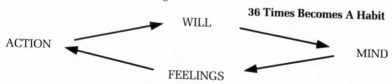

If you have an unloving habit pattern in your life, the following is a plan to change it, so that you can have feelings of love again:

1) Write down a list of those things you consider to be your partner's faults.
2) Go down the list, one by one, and tell God you forgive your partner for each one.
3) Tell God that from now on, all the changing needed in your partner will be His responsibility.

4) When you finish this fault list, ask God to forgive you for judging your partner. Then burn the list. **Don't show it to your partner!**
5) Write down a list of those things you consider to be your partner's good qualities. Keep going until you have 10. There are ten!
6) Go down that list morning and night, and thank God for those good qualities. When you think of another good quality, add it to the list.
7) After doing this for approximately 36 days in a row, you will no longer need the list. You will have started a new habit, a loving habit.
8) Every day, tell your partner you love them, and tell them about one of their good qualities.
9) At least once a week, commit a loving act. Do something for your partner that you know will please them.
10) At least once a week, in front of other people, especially relatives, with your partner present, tell them about one of your partner's good qualities.
11) Spend at least 15 minutes each day in communication; times for sharing each other's thoughts.

If you do the above, feelings of love will be there in your heart.

Remember: we are changing unloving habits in this area, it will take a little while to get used to the new habits. From time to time you may slip back into the old habit. When you do, ask God to forgive you. Ask Him for his supernatural ability to change the habit. Then get started again.

For Further Study of the Scriptures from this Chapter:

I Corinthians 13
John 12:24
Colossians 3:12-15
John 13:1-17

Romans 12:1-2
I John 1:9
Romans 5:5

Chapter Six

God's Plan
For Our Sexuality
(Love Relationships on three Levels)

"And the very God of peace sanctify you wholly; and I pray God your whole spirit and soul and body be preserved blameless unto the coming of our Lord Jesus Christ." (I Thessalonians 5:23 KJV).

Body, Soul and Spirit

I'll bet that you didn't know that you are three people! Well, you are certainly made up of three distinct parts: body, soul and spirit. God is Father, Son and Holy Spirit, and we are made up of body, soul and spirit.

God wants you to have a love relationship on all of these levels.

Remember the Biblical word for spiritual love: "agape". Paul wrote, "The love of God is shed abroad in your hearts by the Holy Spirit.". (Romans 5:5 KJV). There is something wrong with our spirit before we find God. Jesus was referring to this when He told Nicodemus that "you must be born again." He was talking about a very important part of our nature.

Our spirit does not truly come alive until it comes in contact with our Creator. The only way that happens is to accept what Jesus did for us on the cross at Calvary. When we make Jesus the Lord of our lives, we become a new creature in Christ. The Bible says, "If any man be in Christ, he is a new creature: old things are passed away; behold, all things have become new." (2 Corinthians 5:17 KJV). The Bible says that before you become a new creature, your spirit is dead.

"And you hath He quickened, who were dead in trespasses and sins; Wherein in time past ye walked according to the course of this world, according to the prince of the power of the air, the spirit that now worketh in the child of disobedience: Among whom also we all had our conversation in times past in the lusts of our flesh, fulfilling the desires of the flesh and of the mind; and were by nature the children of wrath, even as others." (Ephesians 2:1-3 KJV). This is the Apostle Paul's description of the spirit of man in our sin-born state.

Self-Destructive

Did you know that psychiatrists and psychologists have discovered that we all have a tendency toward suicide? Everyone has an inner urge to self-destruction! It is especially obvious in teenagers. This is true because our spirits are on "self-destruct"! And your spirit remains in this state until it comes in contact with its Creator. But when we accept Jesus as Lord and Saviour our spirit comes alive.

In order for a wholesome love relationship to happen, our spirit has to come alive to our Creator. Often, after someone accepts Christ as Saviour, they say that everything looks brighter: "The sun shines brighter, the trees look greener, and life is better!" This is because their spirit has come alive to God. When your spirit comes alive to God, divine love begins to flow from God to your spirit. You are aware that God loves you. You pray to Him, and He answers; you read your Bible and God's word comes alive! The world looks altogether different. And the in-born tendency to self-destruction is gone. Many people say, "I felt so empty. There was such a void in me until I found Jesus, but now my spirit has come alive!"

This difference betwen a believer whose spirit is alive, and an unbeliever who has not known this experience, is vitally important as we build our relationships. The Bible says: "Be ye not unequally yoked together with unbelievers: for what fellowship hath righteousness with unrighteousness? and what communion hath light with darkness? And what concord hath Christ with Belial? or what part hath he that believeth with an infidel?" (II Corinthians 6:14,15). This King James term, "infidel", simply means someone who is not alive in his or her spirit. Their spirit is on "self-destruct", while yours is alive. Any relationship between the two will mean a real spiritual battle. Their spirit is under the control of this world heading for destruction, while yours is alive in Christ.

This passage continues: "and what agreement hath the temple of God with idols? for ye are the temple of the living God: as God hath said, I will dwell with them, and walk in them; and I will be their God, and they shall be my people." (II Corinthians 6:16 KJV).

A Recipe for Strife

If you marry a non-believer, there is constant strife in the spirit. You may have a good love relationship in other areas, but in the spirit there is war.

Spiritual Dynamite!

I have known many Christians who have divine love flowing from them; they pray and they talk to God, and you know that their spirits are alive. Their partner is the same. But nothing is flowing from partner to partner. They don't pray together; they don't read the Bible together; as a matter of fact, they don't ever talk about spiritual things. They argue that "My relationship with God is a very personal thing."

If a Christian husband and a Christian wife have not made a habit of praying together or reading the Bible together, it can be the hardest thing in the world to start. I am convinced this is because the devil fights this more than anything else. If he can keep you from praying together, he will have accomplished a major victory in his battle to cripple you spiritually. He knows something that many Christian couples do not seem to realize: the time you spend reading the Bible and praying together fosters a spiritual communication that is **dynamite!**

In your marriage, what do you do to keep the spiritual love flowing back and forth?

It is vitally important that you be open to one another in the areas of spirituality. Your closest spiritual companion must be your wife or your husband. You need to be able to discuss everything important to you in these areas with your spouse. It is God's desire that your most intimate prayer partner be your marriage partner. But the devil fights hard against this. If you have not been in the habit of praying in the presence of your wife or husband, there is a wall there, ten feet high. And the devil is busy reinforcing that wall with concrete and steel. If you do not pray together, I guarantee that the very thought of reading the Bible together or discussing anything spiritual in front of your partner scares you to death!

You probably have a number of explanations: "I've never been open like that", or "I'm a very private person." There are all kinds of excuses.

But the fact is that the spiritual wall between you and your partner is from the self-destructive spirit of the world, not from the life-giving Spirit of God. It is anchored in bad habits, habits that you need to change. Now, as we have already seen in this book, changing any habit will involve a struggle.

The Habit of Communion

The starting place is to allow divine love to flow. When this channel is open, all other changes will be much easier. Here is how to open that channel: Get an alarm clock. Oh, you probably already have one, but you're not using it right! If you have not been praying and reading the Bible together and discussing spritual things together, you need to make time to start a new habit.

Set the alarm clock for just after the time when the kids are all in bed. When it goes off, turn off the TV, get a Bible, and sit down together. Let me encourage men to take the lead in this. Ask your wife to read a verse that is very important to her. You might want to comment on it, but you do not need to. Let me caution you: don't read verses that are intended to convey a message to your partner! In doing that, you would simply be falling back into the error of trying to change your partner. That's God's job, remember?

God simply wants you to be a husband and wife and to love each other. Begin by reading a scripture that is important to you, one that God has used to speak to you.

A word of warning: maybe one of you has thought for a long time that you should pray and study the Bible together. Please, don't say, "See, I've been trying to tell you to do this all along". The devil wants you to fight, not to love, and he'll use an opportunity like that to turn fellowship into full-scale battle.

After the wife has read a verse, the husband should do the same. Again, you can comment on it, or simply read the verse. Alternate between partners until you have each read approximately seven verses.

Now, husbands, I want you to tell your wife about something which concerns you, and ask her to pray about it. This should be a short prayer, not a long one. You must guard against a feeling of competition in your prayers: trying to prove that you are better at praying than your partner; or feeling inadequate because you think your spouse prays better than you do. God does not hear you because of long prayers of perfectly-chosen words.

I remember a story about a farmer who gave a testimony about prayers. He said that he had said long prayers and short prayers, he had prayed prayers in church and prayers at home. But the best prayer he had ever prayed was when he was standing on his head in a well on the farm. It was "Lord, help me".

God hears short prayers and ungrammatical prayers.

Men, tell your wife about something that concerns you. Wives, pray something like this: "Lord, you know what my husband is worried about. Please give him wisdom in this." Now the wife tells the husband something that is concerning her. The husband prays for her in the same way. Alternate this way, several times.

And what will happen? You will open your spirits up to one another. You are never as vulnerable as when you are praying in front of your wife. The secret places of your heart are open. You may even shed a tear. This sharing will open your spirits one to the other, and there will be a communication that will flow from spirit to spirit. This will happen in no other way.

Jesus said, "If any two agree in anything, it shall be done" (Matthew 18:19). The Bible also warns us that if men do not treat their wives as they should, their prayers will not receive ready answers. Often, the Lord is waiting for the two of you to agree on something. But what usually happens is that she is praying, "Change him, Lord, change him", while he is praying "Change her, Lord, change her." The power in prayer, and the changes in your relationship, will come when you agree together in prayer. As you share together, God will greatly bless your relationship, and will answer your prayers.

My mom and dad do this twice a day. They share together for half an hour in the morning and for half an hour at night. Dad will mention something and Mom will pray; then Mom will mention something and Dad will pray. It takes them half an hour because they have eight children, and they pray for each one of them. It may be enough for you to spend ten minutes each time. It doesn't have to be a long time, but once you establish that good habit, you will never want to miss it. It will cause Jesus to come right into the middle of your relationship. It will cause divine love to flow from one to the other. It will cause your spirit to come alive. It will give you an ability to communicate together that will amaze you.

Fileo Love

God also cares very much that your marriage relationship include what the Bible calls "Fileo", or friendship love. One of the greatest examples of fileo love is the relationship between David and Jonathan. "And it came to pass, when he had made an end of speaking unto Saul, that the soul of Jonathan was knit with the soul of David, and Jonathan loved him as his own soul. And Saul took him that day, and would let him go no more home to his father's house. Then Jonathan and David made a covenant, because he loved him as his own soul." (I Samuel 18:1-3 KJV).

Elsewhere in the Bible David says that the love he had with Jonathan was better than the love he had with any woman. Some people say that this shows they were homosexuals. This isn't true; the Bible is referring here to friendship love.

Do you know why David never had a closer friendship than this with any of his wives? Because he had many wives and concubines and all of them were angry with him. They had to be; they were a poor, neglected bunch of women. You men have a full-time job ministering to one wife; loving and communicating with one woman is enough responsibility for any man. Can you imagine David's situation, with hundreds of wives and concubines all angry with him? No wonder he was thankful for a friend! Multiple wives was always a heathen custom; it was never God's plan for His people. It always causes a lot of suffering.

Establishing Friendship

Proverbs 18:24 tells us how to establish a loving, friendship relationship: "A man that hath friends must show himself friendly: and there is a friend that sticketh closer than a brother." That "friend" could be Jesus, or it could refer to your husband and wife relationship. It is God's will that you be married to your closest friend. If you are going to live with someone all of your life, it might as well be your best friend. I tell people who are planning to be married that they have to develop the spiritual love relationship, and they have to develop a friendship.

What is a friend? A friend is someone with whom you love to share everything. If there is anything that is important to you, you want to talk it over with that person. I'm reminded of young people in school: they spend all day at school with their friend, but the minute they are home from school they get on the phone to that friend. They love to share. Every idea, every plan, every dream is more exciting as you share it with a friend.

How do you establish such friendships? You must spend time together, communicating. Think of what it is like when a friend moves away, and then you encounter them again after a number of years. What a difference there is in that friendship! It is like you are strangers again.

I've seen married couples who live in the same house acting like those former friends who are now strangers. It isn't that they married the wrong person; but they never cultivated a friendship. A friendship that may have been there in the early days of their relationship was allowed to die. It was not nurtured.

Our individualistic society works against friendship relationships. Everybody does their own thing, and your life is so full of individual pursuits that you have no time to share. This will destroy a marriage, but the situation seems to be part of the reality of life. Time to build a friendship will never suddenly be available to you. Instead, you have to make a plan!

Exclusive Time for your Partner

Here is my suggestion to keep the friendship alive in your relationship: at least once a week, for the rest of your lives, go out and do something together, without the children. Go on a date. Go shopping. Go out to dinner.

Listen, men: before you were married, you took that lady to the places she likes to go. Now, you want to take her only to the places you like to go! I have heard men say, "Sure, I take my wife out. I play hockey every Thursday night and she comes and watches me." What I recommend is that you take her to places she likes, to do things she likes to do. Of course, she can also go with you to places you like as well. Sometimes these times together can be as simple as a walk through the neighbourhood, talking together, or stopping at a restaurant for coffee and conversation. Vary the events, but make it a habit to spend that time together, just the two of you, once a week, every week.

And, although this may surprise you, church doesn't count. Of course, go to church, but you must also have this time, each week, in which you focus only on each other. You have to keep that friendship alive.

It is important to realize that, in the Bible times, the economy was based on family farms or family businesses. Mom and Dad were always there, working together, side by side. It was great for the children — they would work with them as well. The whole family was together. That is God's plan for the family.

In our industrial society, we have taken the man out of the home and put him in the factory. And in our day of working couples, we have taken the woman out of the home, and put her in an office. Man and woman are no longer sharing their life together. We must develop a plan to counter this negative influence. Planning one shared event each week is a good start.

Plan Your Shared Time

One reason that this planning is so important has to do with what happens to a man after he is married. Once a man has a wife, he feels the responsibility to be the provider for that family. He begins to realize his sense of self-worth through his work, from achievement on the job. If a husband receives his self-worth from work, he may focus only on his job, and neglect his wife. When the woman is unable to share in this important part of her husbands's life, she may try to achieve self-worth the same way. She enters the work force, and fights in the market place. But she becomes afraid and angry. A business career is not the whole answer for a woman. It may be worthwhile, but it is not a substitute for a shared relationship within marriage.

A husband and wife need to be walking side by side, sharing together. You must work at fostering that special relationship. Go out together at least once a week. Spend at least 15 minutes each night talking to one another, as friends. Turn the stupid TV off. If you spend all of your time watching TV, it will seriously cripple both your mind and your marriage.

Remember this: as you learn to communicate, always do so in love. Strive to be genuinely interested in your partner's point of view. Avoid attacking one another — as soon as you attack a friend, that friend ceases to be a friend and becomes an enemy.

Eros

The third aspect of the love relationship in marriage is "eros" — erotic, sexual love. This is a major theme of the Song of Solomon.

God created our sexuality, and He is really the only one who knows why it was created and how it should function. And since He created us as three-part beings, to love in three distinct ways, the only time our sexual relationships will function properly is when spiritual love is flowing and friendship love is operating in our marriages. When eros is included in a relationship already based in agape and fileo love, the relationship is wonderfully complete, following God's pattern. We need this complete-ness. You need to share your total intimate self in a life-time love relationship with a member of the opposite sex. Only this will meet your needs.

Sexual Suicide

In our society, we try to meet those needs in many other ways. The devastation that occurs when we depart from God's order is horrendous. This is the primary reason why our mental hospitals are full. We have not found sexual freedom, but sexual suicide! I thank God that He can heal when you come to him crippled, because most of the problems that are encountered in the sexual area are caused because people have moved outside of God's principles for sexual relationships.

God and Sex

How does God feel about your sexuality? There are many people who feel that their sexuality is sinful. They believe that if they are going to be truly spiritual, they cannot enjoy their sexuality. Really spiritual people will not have those kind of desires. I talked to one woman who told me that when she and her husband were sexually intimate, she would take the picture of Jesus that hung in the bedroom, and turn it, face to the wall. She didn't want Jesus to watch them having sex. And unfortunately this is the way many, many people feel. The devil encourages this: he wants you to believe that sexuality is dirty.

Let me state this clearly: sexuality is not dirty. It only becomes corrupt when we act in this area outside of God's principles. The New Testament says, "Marriage is honourable in all, and the bed undefiled: but whoremongers and adulterers God will judge." (Hebrews 13:4 KJV). This word "bed" simply means intimate activity that takes place in the privacy of the bedroom between husband and wife. It is pure and without defilement — holy. There is no sin in it. Some teach that the original sin was not the eating of the forbidden fruit, but the first sex act between Adam and Eve. This is neither Biblical nor true.

I am glad that God is not ashamed of our sexuality. God is not at all ashamed of the genital parts of your body. He created your body to take part in sexual functions, and He is delighted with this. The devil would like you to think of something as sinful, which is really very normal and a proper part of being a God-created person. You are meant to be spiritual _and_ sexual, at the same time!

The scriptures prove that the original sin was not the sex act. The Bible says, "So God created man in His own image, in the image of God created He him; male and female created He them." (Geneis 1:27,28 KJV). Woman are just as much "made in the image of God" as men are! There is no need for the nonsense of changing terms that refer to God into female terms — He is already everything that a woman is, and everything that a man is. Male and female were created in God's image!

"And God blessed them, and God said unto them, Be fruitful, and multiply, and replenish the earth, and subdue it." (Genesis 1:28 KJV). Here they are, in the Garden of Eden, with no sin. But as soon as God created them, He said, 'Here is what the sex act is all about'. He told them to multiply. If God commanded this, will He then turn around and say that it is sin? The devil would like you to think that what is good, is sin; and what is sinful, is good! But God is not inconsistent. Genesis 2:24-25 explains, "Therefore shall a man leave his father and his mother, and shall cleave unto his wife: and they shall be one flesh. And they were both naked, the man and the wife, and were not ashamed." This is all before the fall into sin was ever mentioned.

This word, "naked", is used again in Leviticus where it speaks of a man going in and uncovering the nakedness of his wife; this refers to the intimate, sex relationship. Adam and Eve were participating in the sex act, and they were not ashamed, nor had they yet sinned. Shame comes with sin.

Not only for Procreation

God told Adam and Eve to have sex in order to have children. But this is not the only Biblical reason for sexual intimacy, even though some teach this. Some insist that couples should only have sex when they are trying to have children; when they are not trying to have children, they should abstain.

This is certainly not what Paul teaches in I Corinthians: "Nevertheless, to avoid fornication, let every man have his own wife, and let every woman have her own husband. Let the husband render unto the wife due benevolence: and likewise also the wife unto the husband. The wife hath not power of her own body, but the husband: and likewise the husband hath not power of his own body, but the wife. Defraud ye not one the other, except it be with consent for a time, that ye may give yourselves to fasting and prayer; and come together again, that

Satan tempt you not for you incontinency." (I Corinthians 7:2-5 KJV).

Let me also quote the Living Bible rendition of this passage: "Usually it is best to be married, each man having his own wife and each woman having her own husband because otherwise you might fall back into sin. The man should give his wife all that is her right as a married woman and the woman should do the same for her husband."

It is not only a matter of the wife meeting the husband's needs. This is important; and we need to realize that the woman's needs are very much different.

"For a girl who married no longer has full right to her own body, for her husband has rights to it too. So in the same way the husband no longer has full right to his own body, for it belongs also to the wife. So do not refuse these rights to each other. The only exception to the rule would be the agreement of both husband and wife to refrain from the rights of marriage for a limited time so that they can give themselves more completely to prayer. Afterwards they should come together again so that Satan won't be able to tempt them because of their lack of self-control.".

Basic Intimate Needs

Do you see what God is saying in these verses? He says that the man and the woman have basic intimate needs. Your sexual drive is your strongest need, and it is ordained by God. You need to share intimately in a total sexual love relationship; to be fulfilled with one another all of your life.

Because this relationship is God's idea, He is eager to instruct you as to how to know one another and to meet one another's needs. Ask God for His help in this. The devil hates it when Christian couples who love the Lord have a beautiful sex relationship. He wants to divert you into sinful areas, because then he can really cripple you. But God realizes that you have a need for intimacy. He commands married couples to meet one another's needs, because if this is not taking place, you will leave yourself open for temptation.

Incidentally, did you notice anything about children in this passage? If the only reason for sex was to have children, surely reproduction would have been mentioned here — but it is not. Instead, Paul is teaching that, apart from producing babies, people have a basic sexual need.

Large sections of the book of Proverbs are devoted to the subject of sex. Notice Proverbs 5:18-20: "Let thy fountain be blessed: and rejoice with the wife of thy youth. Let her be as the loving hind and the pleasant roe; let her breasts satisfy thee at all times; and be thou ravished always with her love. And why wilt thou, my son, be ravished with a strange woman and embrace the bosom of a stranger?"

This whole chapter is dedicated to sexuality. It is the instruction of a father to a son, warning him of the terrible things that will happen to a young man who goes to bed with harlots. The father tells his son to keep his sexuality within marriage. Those verses also tell us one of the other reasons God gave us our sexuality: pleasure. God's plan is that sexual intimacy will supply one of life's greatest, most pleasurable experiences for both the man and the woman.

Pleasure: God's Creation

Did you know that the devil did not create pleasure? Your ability to enjoy pleasure owes nothing to the devil. God created pleasure. God made you so that there are parts of your sexuality that are only there to give you a pleasurable experience. Isn't God good? There have been some religions and some cultures that have tried to separate sexual experience from pleasure, by attempting to deny pleasure. But Jesus said, "In my presence is fullness of joy and at my right hand are pleasures forevermore" (Psalm 16:11). Every pleasure was given to us by God, but pleasure must be enjoyed within His rules. God's plan, concerning sexuality, was to give you one of life's greatest pleasures. God is not at all ashamed of what happens between a husband and a wife in the privacy of your bedroom.

The Sexuality of the Song of Solomon

Let's look at the seventh chapter of the Song of Solomon. This is a very important passage, because it counteracts the "dirtying" of sexual intimacy that the devil has tried to accomplish. If a person — especially a woman — associates sex with something dirty it will do great harm to a marriage relationship.

Unless you — again, especially if you are a woman — associate sexual intimacy with purity and love and other beautiful things, your body will not respond. A man also needs to make these associations with purity, love, commitment and faithfulness to one woman, or else he cripples himself.

In this chapter of the Song of Solomon we hear a conversation between the king and his new queen on their wedding night, just before they enter into intimate relationships. How pure is this act? Well, throughout the book it uses this relationship as a comparison to the relationship between Christ and His Church. God wanted to show us something beautiful and intimate and precious about His relationship to us. He used the sexual relationship between a husband and wife, and said, "This is a picture of what you are to Me! You are My bride! I am your husband. One day we are going to be together at the Marriage Supper of the Lamb." This is how beautiful and special He feels you are to Him. Let's read Song of Solomon 7:1-13:

"How beautiful are your tripping feet, O queenly maiden. Your rounded thighs are like jewels, the work of the most skilled of craftsmen. Your navel is lovely as a goblet filled with wine. Your waist is like a heap of wheat set about with lilies. Your two breasts are like two fawns, yes, lovely twins." Perhaps I need to remind you that I am quoting from the Bible. I'm quite sure you have never heard this passage from the pulpit on a Sunday morning!

We treat the Bible as if God is ashamed of sex. But the Bible is filled with sex! Here, Solomon is looking at his bride's naked body and telling her how delighted he is!

I once heard a woman giving a "super-spiritual" testimony. She said, "My husband and I got married twenty years ago and he has never seen my body above the knees." I said, "Oh God, help her!" She thought this was a very spiritual thing. But she was denying one of God's good gifts. It is God who has given sexuality to you, to be experienced with your partner, anointed by the Lord and dedicated to Jesus.

Solomon is obviously looking at her when he says, "Your two breasts are like two fawns, yes, lovely twins. Your neck is stately as an ivory tower, your eyes as limpid pools in Heshbon by the gate of Bath-rabbim. Your nose is shapely like the tower of Lebanon overlooking Damascus." A woman really needs to feel that her man cherishes every part of her body. Her whole being delights in this. Here, Solomon is communicating that kind of appreciation.

"As Mount Carmel crowns the mountains, so your hair is your crown. The king is held captive in your queenly tresses. Oh, how delightful you are; how pleasant, O love, for utter delight. You are tall and slim like a palm tree, and your breasts are like its clusters of dates." He likens her body to a palm tree, a fruit tree, and then becomes very explicit:

"I said, I will climb up into the palm tree and take hold of its branches. Now may your breasts be like grape clusters, and the scent of your breath like apples, and your kisses as exciting as the best of wine, smooth and sweet, causing the lips of those who are asleep to speak."

He tells his love that her sexuality is very exciting. It would awaken a man from a dead sleep! Then she replies to him:

"I am my beloved's and I am the one he desires. Come, my beloved, let us go out into the fields and stay in the villages. Let us get up early and go out to the vineyards and see whether the vines have budded and whether the blossoms have opened and whether the pomegranates are in flower." She likens her body to a fruit garden. She asks her lover to be patient, and then tells him that she will give him her love.

"There the mandrakes give forth their fragrance and the rarest fruits are at our doors." Do you get this? This is not just a woman meeting a man's needs; this is an excursion into great pleasure for both man and woman! I have known women who have been married for many years, and never once has the sex act been pleasurable for them. That is a shame.

". . . the new as well as old, for I have stored them up for my beloved." Isn't this delightful? Isn't this a beautiful picture of intimacy? The Bible is packed with images like this; a great celebration of the godly pleasure of marital intimacy.

Two as One: A Spiritual Bonding

Let me show you something else that happens when you come together as a couple.

Perhaps you thought, as you stood before the minister on your wedding day, that as you repeated your vows you became man and wife. Actually, what you were doing was asking God's blessing on something you were about to do that night. The following passage from Paul's letter was written because the Christians were asking, "Is it all right to go to bed with a harlot, because all of the heathen religions are doing it?" Free sex is not new, you know. There is no new morality, just old immorality that has been with us as long as man has been on the face of this earth! Paul answered their question in very strong terms: "What? Know ye not that he which is joined to a harlot is one body? for two, said he, shall be one flesh." (I Corinthians 6:16 KJV).

When a man and a woman have sex together there is a bond that takes place, a spiritual union. You will never be quite the same again. As a matter of fact, a man who goes from one woman to another woman soon loses his ability to bond with one. Unless he receives an inner healing, he will find that shortly after he is married, he will be greatly drawn to other women.

When you come together sexually, you become one. It is commonly known that a woman changes when she loses her virginity. Her attitude toward herself changes: she looks different and feels different. Something spiritual has happened! There is a record in heaven that these two have become one. Every time you come together with your spouse there is a declaration in heaven. Your intimacy is a recommitment of your marriage. It is a declaration, to one another, that you are one. God likens it to the commitment He has made to the church. We are one.

There have been cultures in which the sexual union of husband and wife happened before the marriage ceremony was completed. They would go to bed immediately before the ceremony ended, and then come out as husband and wife. In our society, we wait for the wedding night. Of course, the sad reality is, in our society we don't wait at all. By the time a man comes to be married, he is bonded to so many women that he doesn't know who his wife is and is driven with emotional confusion. He becomes married, and is confused because he doesn't really know who his wife is; he feels no bond, no commitment. God

116

can help this. Aren't you glad? He can bring you back into His will and His plan, into the only way that your intimate needs will be met in a way that is right and holy.

The Bible plainly teaches that sexual intimacy is given to us by God, within the marriage context, for a number of beautiful reasons. It fulfills the need to share your total intimate self with a member of the opposite sex, for the rest of your life. It gives you one of life's great pleasurable experiences. It makes you one, uniting bodies, souls and spirits together. There is a flowing together. It consumates a marriage.

In the midst of this beautiful intimacy we sometimes lock hands with our Creator and there is created an immortal living soul! Jesus said that this new life created through sexual union is of more value than the whole universe.

God created the universe, and the earth, so He could have us. Then He created Adam and Eve from the dust. God loves to share His creative ability with us. He devised a plan so that we can cooperate in the creation of the most beautiful creature he ever created. He designed the plan to work as we are together in unity. He plants immortal living souls in the midst of that creative act between husband and wife.

In loving, and consumating the marriage, from one of life's greatest pleasures comes forth a living soul for whom Jesus died. When that person accepts Jesus, he or she becomes joint heir with Christ, and will rule and reign with Him throughout eternity. This one created by the union of groom and bride will become a member of the Bride of Christ. Jesus cares for His Bride.

Do not ever think that your sexuality is evil. God made it, He loves it, and He has a wonderful plan for you and your sexuality. Your sexuality is the heart of your creativity. Most of what you do as a man or a woman is very much linked to your sexuality. It is the heart of your emotional stability.

Three Love Relationships

God wants you to have three love relationships with your partner. He wants you to be married to your closest spiritual partner (agape love). He wants you to walk through life with your closest friend (fileo love). And He wants you to celebrate his great gift of sexuality with your husband or wife (eros love).

117

Principles
For Healthy Relationships

God's Plan For Friendship Love (Fileo)

Friendship Love (Fileo) requires time spent in sharing with one another.

1) One night each week must be set aside for husband and wife without your children.
2) At least 15 minutes each day must be set aside to sit down and talk to . . . and listen to . . . each other.

God's Plan For Agape Love

Godly, divine love (Agape) is kept alive through spiritual communion one with another.

1) The husband and wife must have private times of prayer and reading God's word, together.
2) If you haven't been praying and reading the Bible together, here is a summary of our plan for beginning this spiritual habit:
   a) Set your alarm clock to get you up early enough to have time to share together.
   b) Let the man take the lead in sharing.
   c) The wife is to read a verse that is important to her. You can comment on it, but this is not necessary.
   d) The husband is to do the same.
   e) Alternate this way until you have read about seven verses each.
   f) The husband is to now tell the wife something which concerns him, and ask her to pray about it.
   g) The wife is to pray for her husband in this matter. It should be a short, simple prayer.
   h) The wife does the same, and the husband prays for her.
   i) Alternate this way, several times.
   j) Make this a daily habit.

God's Plan For Our Sexuality (Eros Love)

Everyone has the need to share his or her total intimate self in a lifetime love relationship with a member of the opposite sex.

1) The sexual activity in the marriage bedroom is without sin (Hebrews 13:4).
2) The man and the woman have basic intimate needs. You need to share intimately in a total sexual love relationship, to be fulfilled with one another all your life (I Corinthians 7:2-5).
3) God's plan is that sexual intimacy will supply one of life's greatest, most pleasurable experiences for both the man and the woman (Proverbs 5:18-20; Song of Solomon 7).
4) When a man and a woman have sex together, a bond is created — a spiritual union. It is this act which makes you one (I Corinthians 6:16).
5) Sometimes, a husband and wife join hands with our Creator to create an immortal living soul (Psalm 127:3-5).

For Further Study of the Scriptures from this Chapter:

I Thessalonians 5:23	Proverbs 18:24
Romans 5:5	Hebrews 13:4
II Corinthians 5:17	Genesis 1:27-28; 2:24-25
Ephesians 2:1-3	I Corinthians 6:16; 7:2-5
II Corinthians 6:14-16	Proverbs 5:18-20
Matthew 18:19	Psalm 16:11; 127:3-5
I Samuel 18:13	Song of Solomon 7

Chapter Seven

Sexuality

In a previous chapter, I quoted briefly from Proverbs 5. I want to return to this important section, which deals at length with sexuality, so that we can study together some additional, important Biblical truths. This entire chapter is focused on sexuality. In it, the Holy Spirit talks to us as though we were a young teenager, and He gives us some very practical information concerning our sexuality. And who should know better that the Lord? The Holy Spirit was there at the time of creation, and He should know how He made us!

The passage is important enough that I am going to quote all of Proverbs 5, from the Living Bible:

"Listen to me, my son! I know what I am saying: listen! Watch yourself, lest you be indiscreet and betray some vital information. For the lips of a prostitute are as sweet as honey, and smooth flattery is her stock in trade. But afterwards only a bitter conscience is left to you, sharp as a double-edged sword. She leads you down to death and hell. For she does not know the path to life. She staggers down a crooked trail, and doesn't even realize where it leads.

"Young men, listen to me, and never forget what I'm about to say: Run from her!".

The Attack of Immorality

Let me interject to suggest this: you could turn this around and could be talking to a young girl. Immoral women lead men astray, and immoral men lead women astray. As soon as you are involved in immorality, you begin to lead the innocent astray. A prostitute, a promiscuous man or a promiscuous woman, does not want another promiscuous person. They go after the virgin or the faithful husband or faithful wife. They pursue them, and after they have taken them, they lose interest in that one, and go after another. The devil uses their sexuality for great crippling and breaking up of families.

"Young men, listen to me, and never forget what I'm about to say: Run from her! Don't go near her house, lest you fall to her temptation and lose your honor, and give the remainder of your life to the cruel and merciless; lest strangers obtain your wealth, and you become a slave of foreigners. Lest afterwards you groan in anguish and shame, when syphilis consumes your body, and you say, 'Oh, if only I had listened. If only I had not demanded my own way! Oh, why wouldn't I take advice? Why was I so stupid? For now I must face public disgrace.'

"Drink from your own well, my son — be faithful and true to your wife. Why should you beget children with women of the street? Why share your children with those outside your home? Let your manhood be a blessing; rejoice in the wife of your youth. Let her charms and tender embrace satisfy you. Let her love alone fill you with delight. Why delight yourself with prostitutes, embracing what isn't yours? For God is closely watching you, and he weighs carefully everything you do.

"The wicked man is doomed by his own sins; they are ropes that catch and hold him. He shall die because he will not listen to the truth; he has let himself be led away into incredible folly."

The Reasons for the Rules

This is very plain, isn't it? The loving heavenly Father is letting us in on the reasons for the rules.

This is far different from the message of the world: "Be sexually free. We're no longer in the Victorian age. We can express ourselves sexually." The devil went into business in the garden of Eden, as he lied to Eve. He is still in the same business! Over and over again through the media, on television and in movies, we are told and shown that illicit sex is normal. In our schools, our young people are taught birth control in such a way that they believe the time to start is now, all in the name of free sexual expression. This is occurring at the ages of 13 and 14!

Attack on Christianity

Christianity has become the villain, because Biblical teachings are blamed for inhibiting people sexually! Christianity stands accused by secular humanists, who are trying to teach the children to be uninhibited.

My children have just come out of high school, so I have a good idea about what is happening there. I have talked to teachers and a lot of students. Do you know that if your child is fifteen and still a virgin, not only do the rest of the students in the classroom laugh at them, but so do the teachers? They are told to grow up: "Are you going to be a baby all your life?" As a matter of fact, they will be accused of being gay. This may not be true in every classroom, but it is in a surprising number of them.

We have come to a place where young people do not feel that they are normal unless they are sleeping around. Young men feel that if they turn down an opportunity, they are less than a man. But here, in Proverbs, our heavenly Father is giving clear instructions which go completely against the spirit of our age. He makes it plain that your sexuality is very special within marriage. If you take your sexuality outside of that God-given area, it will devastate you terribly. A promiscuous lifestyle will completely mess you up, emotionally, and quite probably, physically!

God tells us, also in Proverbs, "But whoso committeth adultery with a woman lacketh understanding." (Proverbs 6:32 KJV). In other words, if you really knew what you were doing, and the grief it will bring, you would not do it! "He that doeth it destroyeth his own soul."

When God gave these rules He was acting for your good. He is not a sadist looking to torture you. He did not place an immense emotional drive in you only to remove any opportunity to fulfill it. He's not like that.

God is Protecting You

In I Corinthians 6:13, He tells us what our bodies are for: "Now the body is not for fornication". The Corinthians had asked if it was permissible to have sex with a harlot or to sleep around with different partners. The Holy Spirit, speaking

123

through Paul, said, "NO!" But this was not because God wanted to spoil the fun, but because such activity would spoil the people involved! He, the Creator, should know — He did not make your body for the purpose of fornication.

Perhaps you have, at some time, purchased a new car. Did you get the manual that came with it? Let's say that you bought the car, but didn't bother to read the manual. You say, "This is my car, and nobody can tell me what to do with it. It's mine. I own it! I have a right to do with it whatever I want." This is how some people talk about their sexuality: "Don't tell me how to handle my sexuality. I can live promiscuously if I want to. If I want to love somebody, I will. If I want to have an abortion, I will. I belong to me!" But God knows how He made you.

Let's get back into the car. You say, "Since it's my car, I'm going to do whatever I want. I'm going to drive across Lake Ontario, and nobody is going to tell me I can't."

A few minutes later, you walk, dripping wet, back up onto the beach, and complain: "That car is no good. The manufacturers must be crazy. I'm going to get another car, and drive across that lake!" Your body is no more made for promiscuity than that car was to drive across the lake. God has given us His Word as our owner's manual for this fantastic creation, our own body. The Bible says a great deal about your sexuality, because it is so important. One thing it says is, "Flee fornication. Every sin that a man doeth is without the body; but he that committeth fornication sinneth against his own body." (I Corinthians 6:18 KJV). You will damage your own body. Nothing will hurt you more than sexual sin.

Man's Practice/God's Purpose

Perhaps you are thinking, "What about David and those other men in the Bible. They had many wives; what about that?" I can assure you, multiple wives (or husbands) have never been God's plan. In fact, He spoke against it. In God's law, you can read: "Neither shall he (the king of Israel) multiply wives to himself, that his heart turn not away." (Deuteronomy 17:17 KJV). It was a heathen custom that the Biblical characters adopted, to their own harm. It caused havoc wherever it appeared.

124

God Wants You to Have Enjoyment

Or maybe you are thinking, "Lorne is trying to take all the fun out of life." Let me assure you: I'm not. Instead, I believe that God knows where the real fun is! He doesn't want to take the fun out of your life; He wants to give great enjoyment and pleasure to you! It is the devil who wants to rob you.

The world will tell you that if you have a lot of experiences with different partners before you are married, you will be an experienced sex partner when you marry your spouse. Many people have said to me, "I had no sex experiences before I was married. I wonder if that is normal." I say, "Thank God!" Surveys had found that those people that have the most fulfilling sex lives are those who waited until they were married, who came together for the first time on their wedding night. An extensive survey carried out by non-Christians in the 1970's found that people who live their lives by Judaeo-Christian principles have the happiest sex lives. They participate in sex with their spouse more often than other people, and receive more pleasure and fulfillment.

These experts found that unless a woman has the commitment of marriage, she feels vulnerable and begins to feel used. She pulls away from the closeness of the relationship, and finds less enjoyment in her sexuality. It seems that there is something in her needing the assurance that the man will never leave her. She needs to know that he will always love her and cherish her above all else. If she has these assurances, her sexuality comes to life and she finds it very easy to respond to such a man. This survey suggested that this might be related to the fact that she bears children.

I said, "Thank you Jesus, you know what you are doing!"

Men who sleep with women to whom they are not married, tend not to respect those women. In a very short period of time the man begins to feel the relationship is meaningless. He leaves her and looks for another girl, and then waits until he has married her, before they sleep together!

The Need For Commitment

The survey suggested this is partially because there is a need in a man to make a commitment, and to be responsible for the children. If a woman doesn't ask for such a commitment, he doesn't respect her. It was suggested that this attitude is very evident in the names men use for women who have sex with many men. Men have terrible names for promiscuous women, all around the world: sluts, whores, and far worse! Men, for some reason, hate prostitutes. Prostitutes, for some reason, hate men! See what the devil is doing?

The Evil Results of Promiscuity

Promiscuity has no good results. A promiscuous man will find that he does not like women! He has a hidden, subconscious anger toward women. This is a major reason for the incredible number of rapes in our society, and for the horrible fact of wife abuse. I have found that in most cases, a man who beats his wife is also a man who sleeps around. This is wonderful sexual freedom?

I have talked to men who have gone from woman to woman. They are nervous wrecks. You show me a promiscuous man, and I'll show you an emotionally insecure man, a man who hates himself and doesn't even know why! There is healing for that, but until that happens, he will never be able to love a woman because you cannot love a woman unless you love yourself.

A man told me, "I went to a psychiatrist because I'm awfully hard on myself." The psychiatrist told him it was an emotional problem. As we talked together, I discovered why. He had been promiscuous since he was a little boy. He married his first wife because he had made her pregnant. After having a couple of children with her, he began to run around, and got another girl pregnant. He did not fulfill the role of father at all in this new relationship. He left his wife, slept around, and two other women became pregnant by him. Then he began a steady relationship with a girl, got her pregnant, and left.

I asked him, "What was your Dad like?" He said, "He was a good man."

I asked, "Did your Dad ever run around on your Mom?" He said no. I asked how he would have felt if he would have seen his Dad in bed with another woman.

"Oh," he said, "I would have died."

I asked him, "And that is what is wrong with you. Every time you look at your children, you hate yourself; every time you think of them, you hate yourself." He said, "That's true".

I told him that he needed to settle down and be husband and father, and take the responsibility for that relationship, and for that family. And I told him that God would only be able to help him if he confessed what he had done as sin.

What had happened to this man? He had accepted Hollywood's lie that a true man was a macho-man. He had been-crippled. That view of man only produces a bunch of animals who hate themselves, and hate women. The Bible calls it, being "without natural affection."

The Purpose Of A Man's Sexuality

Sexuality is supposed to motivate you to be husband and father; to be willing to die for that woman! If you have been promiscuous, unless you receive healing from the Lord, you will be unable to fulfill these things.

I remember one man, who had been a Christian for two years, who told me, "Lorne, I have this terrible problem. I can't look at a woman without undressing her in my mind. If I'm talking to a woman, I don't even hear what she is saying; I just see her with her clothes off. I'm trying to be a Christian, but this thing comes over me in waves. I shared it with my wife, but the devastation that came over her face was as though I had run a sword through her."

This was his third wife. As we talked, I discovered that he had begun to be promiscuous at the age of fifteen; he started with a 45 year old woman. That is what headed him down this path. He should have listened to what the Word of the Lord said with regard to a prostitute! When he married his first wife, she was pregnant. You see, he was seeing himself as a macho-man, thinking that all his affairs were proof of his manhood. This man had taken a strong, God-given drive, intended for life and love and wholeness, and has used it for perversion. We worked together through this, and prayed. I told him to confess his sin.

127

A Real Man

I want you to realize that a man who seduces women is not a "he-man". Any weak boy can have many affairs. But it takes a man, a real man, to be committed to his wife.

I prayed with this man, and ministered to him, and God wonderfully healed him! He got his emotions back in line.

God wants men to look at their wives and see them as a person, not as a sex object. Sexuality between you and your wife is a beautiful thing, but she will not respond if you think of sex, first. She must be loved first as a person. If you get this out of line, you will lose the ability to love her with natural affection.

Another Christian man came to me after being married for six months. He told me, "I want to know whether I'm normal or not. I go to bed with my wife and I find that I am losing interest in her sexually. She doesn't turn me on at all. As a matter of fact, I find myself looking at other girls all the time and getting excited sexually. The only way I can get sexually interested in my wife is if I imagine that I am with another girl, so I let my mind go and fantasize. Then it happens to me."

Pornography

Some psychologists and psychiatrists approve of this practice. But I don't. Instead, I said, "No, it's not normal. You need a healing." And then I told him, "either you had a lot of affairs with girls before you were married or else you are looking at a lot of pornography right now." Pornography is a big step down the road to promiscuity. It never stirs you up towards your wife; instead, if you watch or read pornography, you are an open candidate for the devil to tempt you into an affair.

The romantic love stories that women read are equivalent to pornography. They lead you just as directly into fantasizing about illicit affairs. You will lose interest in your husband.

I told this young man that he had been involved in affairs or pornography, and he looked at me in surprise: "How did you know?"

I explained that he had all of the signs and all of the scars from this kind of lifestyle, that what had happened to him was a direct result of promiscuity. It is a terrible thing: the world convinces our young people that a promiscuous lifestyle is normal. We are told this so often, through television and music and all kinds of media, that even Christian parents are afraid to tell their young people to remain virgins and avoid promiscuity. But remember, "He that committeth fornication lacks understanding; he destroys his own soul."

I ministered to that man, and he is still with his wife and everything is fine. He needed an inner healing. If he had not dealt with this at the early stage of his marriage, he would have had problems down the road. Promiscuous people lose their ability to bond with their partners, and they develop the habit of not liking the partner they are with. Any woman who has felt for a number of years that she has been used, will enter marriage with negative expectations. She will find it almost impossible to accept her husband's love, even if it is genuine.

Sexual Destruction Of A Woman

A woman's sexuality responds when she associates sex with loving, beautiful things. If she associates sexual union with the surety that "I'm being loved and this is beautiful and this man will never leave me, because he cares for me," her sexuality comes alive.

But if a young teenage girl begins to have sexual experiences in the name of sexual freedom, she will have deep, deep problems. She has her first relationship at 14. Soon, the boy or man leaves her. This will devastate her, because in order for a young girl to give herself for the first time, she has to believe that she has found her man, a man who truly loves her. She believes that she is finally a woman. When a woman gives herself sexually, she gives her whole being. She is the vulnerable one; it is she who bears the children. In order for a woman to enjoy sex, she has to let go, to let down all the barriers, to trust. She becomes completely vulnerable.

That is what this young girl has done; she has trusted a man who will let her down within a week! She has trusted a man who will talk about how easy she was to his friends. Soon she hears those rumours that are flying around, about her! She expresses anger to the man, and he tells her, "Get away from me, you slut!"

Many young girls commit suicide after such an experience. They are devastated. It is hard enough for an adult woman to go through something like this! This is sexual freedom? This is what we are encouraging our children to become involved in?

This girl reaches out again, because she truly wants to be loved. But the guys have heard that she is easy, and they respond to her for a totally different reason. The next guy drops her even sooner. Let's say this happens one hundred times, or two hundred, or three hundred — and don't think these figures are crazy; many young girls have that many encounters — and then she gets married. What has formed her understanding of sexuality? She associates sexuality with being abandoned and rejected, with being gossiped about and being despised.

Over and over again, I have ministered to girls in this situation who have seen all the hurt surface after a year or two of marriage. Suddenly, they can't stand it when their husbands touch them. They find themselves running off to have an affair because if they don't hurt their husband first, he will inevitably hurt them. That's the way it has happened hundreds of times!

Other Dangers

This is the psychological and spiritual hurt that comes from promiscuity in a girl. But there are other dangers, as well. They may contract disease — an incredible number of people in North America now suffer from some kind of disease contracted through sexual contact — or become pregnant. Most girls get pregnant, and it is horrible to realize how many of them quickly get an abortion. Some girls, by the time they reach 21, have had five or six abortions! They don't tell their parents, they just get rid of the baby. This is sexual freedom.?

This girl worries constantly, from the age of 14 until she is married, that she may be pregnant. It is not surprising then, that after she is married she associates pregnancy with fear. She will be unable to respond sexually to her husband, if she is afraid, even subconsciously, of becoming pregnant.

The Evil Of Abortion

Of course, when a girl or a woman has an abortion, there is great potential for emotional harm. Many women need psychi-
130

atric help after they have abortions. Abortion is devastating to the woman who was carrying the child. You see, every cell in her body seeks to protect that child. In fact, God has made a woman in such a way that your entire being calls for you to lay down your life to protect that baby in you; when you go against this, you do violence to your mental and emotional stability.

Women who have had abortions find it very difficult to bond to children born to them later. Because of this, they are more easily upset or irritated by their children, and this can result in child abuse. The same spirit that aborts also abuses. This is sexual freedom? God help us! If any of these stories sound familiar to you, if you have lived a promiscuous life, you need inner healing. And God is eager to bring this to you.

Did David "Get Away With It"?

Perhaps you remember David's adultery, and his multiple wives, and you are wondering, "Why did David get away with it?" Psalm 38:1-11 may answer that question:

"O Lord, rebuke me not in thy wrath: neither chasten me in thy hot displeasure. For thine arrows stick fast in me, and thy hand presseth me sore. There is no soundness in my flesh because of thine anger; neither is there any rest in my bones because of my sin. For mine iniquities are gone over mine head: as an heavy burden they are too heavy for me. My wounds stink and are corrupt because of my foolishness. I am troubled; I am bowed down greatly; I go mourning all day long. For my loins are filled with a loathsome disease; and there is no soundness in my flesh."

Did you notice this? King David was filled with a disease in his private parts.

"I am feeble and sore broken: I have roared by reason of the disquietness of my heart. Lord, all my desire is before thee; and my groaning is not hid from thee. My heart panteth, my strength faileth me: as for the light of mine eyes, it also is gone from me." This is what happens with venereal disease.

"My lovers and my friends stand aloof from my sore; and my kinsmen stand afar off."

131

There is David with many wives and concubines who won't come near him because he has venereal disease. I've heard people say, "Wouldn't it be nice to be like King David or Solomon and have a thousand wives? You could have one whenever you wanted." No, you couldn't. They wouldn't touch him. He was suffering for his sexual law-breaking.

A woman came to me and said, "Lorne, tell me what is wrong with me. I do the meanest things to my husband, even though he is such a good man. Nobody could be a better man than my husband. He is loving and kind, but I know how to hurt him, and I do, unmercifully. I see such pain come into his face. I feel bad about it, and I tell him that I'm sorry, but then I do it again and again and again. What is wrong with me?"

We prayed together, and then I asked her, "When you were a teenage girl, did you have any relationships with guys where you were hurt?" She began to cry like a baby.

She said, "How did you know? I was raised in a Christian church, but when I was sixteen, I started necking heavily with the boy I was dating, and soon we were doing everything. Night after night we would have sex. But one day, he got up and left me and I haven't seen him since. Nobody knows about this. I have nightmares of walking downtown, turning a corner, and seeing him face to face. I dread that. If I ever see him again, I think that I would die."

Now, here she is, twenty years later, married to a good man and making him pay for what happened to her when she was a young teenager. I led her through inner healing, and she was able to forgive her former boyfriend. God wonderfully healed that woman.

Offenses Against Our Youth

We do terrible things to our teenagers. We don't help them out, or offer them any explanations about what is happening to them. We let them sit around in cars necking for hours on end, and then wonder why they get pregnant. We know that adults cannot sit around necking for hours on end without something happening, but we expect our teenagers to handle it. They didn't have such crazy expectations in Bible times. They were much more conscious of chaperoning the young people.

Crippled

I remember a woman who once attended my class on marriage. As I began to talk, she started to shake, and she would get up and leave. When people are crippled in these areas, and you begin to talk about them this is a common response. The pain is too great. She tried to attend those classes — she would come back in, begin to tremble, and then leave again.

She later came to me for counselling, and she told me that she had had a very promiscuous lifestyle. She was now married, but was having a terrible time in her relationship with her husband. But God is so good. He healed her heart, and then He healed her of herpes! Two years later she told me, "Something really beautiful happened. I haven't had a sign of herpes in two years." Jesus heals herpes! There is another cure, as well — one man and one woman for all of your life. But if you have been foolish and sinful in the past and have crippled your sexuality, come to Jesus.

Homosexuality

Do you know why a man becomes a homosexual? At some point in his life he has begun to believe he should have been a woman. It may have started with a mother who wanted a little girl, and dressed her boy up like a girl, and treated him like a girl. It may have been because of a father who abandoned the family. Or perhaps the boy was raised in a home where an alcoholic father beat him. Most homosexuals hate their father.

The boy grows up hearing his mother tell him he is like his father, because she sees the father in him. The little boy reacts in horror, because he has learned to hate his father, and he decides it is not nice to be a boy. During his school-age years, the boy does not have a natural, wholesome relationship with his father. He finds himself doing girlish things because subconsciously he has rejected his maleness and all of the children at school treat him like a sissy.

Remember: whatever you feed your mind, your emotions will prompt your will to fulfill.

The same is true of a lesbian. She has learned to hate her womanhood. Perhaps she is a victim of the extreme doctrines of

133

women's liberation, which teach women to fight men, to protect themselves against men, because men get all the breaks. She began to feel that it was not fair that she was born a woman, and begins to subconsciously reject her womanhood.

Did you know that homosexuals and lesbians are very suicidal? Great depression comes over them. Some might argue that they are suffering the rejection of society, but I believe the truth is, they are trying to kill their identity. You cannot deny your sexuality without trying to kill your identity.

By the time a homosexual or a lesbian reaches the age of 19 or 20, psychologists say that the pattern is set. They cannot change. But I thank God that He can heal! I have seen God heal homosexuals beautifully. The answer is not a sex change; it is a spiritual change.

Healing For Homosexuals And Lesbians

In inner healing, I like to take homosexuals and lesbians right back to the time of conception. I suggest a conversation that was held in heaven: God said, "I want a man. A manchild is what I want," and I suggest that God even called him by name. The same is true of a lesbian: I remind them that God wanted a woman.

It is important to realize that, with very few medical exceptions, your sexuality is centered in your mind. And even in those extreme cases where a child is born with both male and female genitals, their sexuality is still dependent on what is fed into their minds from when they were a child. The secular counsellors who argue that it is too late to change, and then try to help a homosexual to live with his homosexuality, really aren't helping at all. The situation only becomes worse. They become increasingly self-destructive, because they really hate their real gender, and the sexuality they have assumed.

Child Molesting

I counselled a man in his fifties who had molested children all of his life. He had been arrested three times, and was facing ten years in jail. A court-appointed psychiatrist had recommended that he adopt a homosexual lifestyle, because that might resolve some of the tensions. The man told me, "I don't know what comes over me. I just have such an overwhelming urge for children. Afterwards, I hate myself." He told his wife the truth about himself, and he promised not to molest the children, but he did it anyway. His wife charged him, and would have nothing to do with him.

We began to talk about his childhood, and I discovered that from the time he was a little child, he had been molested over and over again by adults. There was incest in his home. Subconsciously, he began to believe that relationships were supposed to take place between adults and children.

He married a woman, and could not respond to her. He told me that when he was 12 years old, he was lying on his bed, nude, and playing with his genitals. His mother caught him, came in with a belt, and whipped him over and over again saying, "You rotten filthy kid. I'll teach you, I'll beat you to death." He had scars from head to foot from that belt. And when he reached adulthood, he could not respond to a woman. And because of being molested, he felt pushed toward children.

I led him through all of this, and he was able to understand why he was the way he was, and to forgive himself and his mother and all those men who molested him. We asked the Lord to heal him, to change all of this around, and to bring his sexual manhood into proper order. It took a long time, as we fought the lies of the devil, but God healed him, and made him a man. He was free! Praise God, the courts did not send him to jail. He is no longer terribly tempted to go after children, and is very active in a church. He contacted his wife and asked her to forgive him.

Aren't you glad that God heals? It doesn't matter what kind of crippling there may have been in the past, Jesus died for that crippling. He died that you might be free. He can heal your sexuality no matter how badly the devil has crippled it.

Paul wrote about this kind of healing: "Know ye not that the unrighteous shall not inherit the kingdom of God? Be not deceived: neither fornicators, nor idolaters, nor adulterers, nor effeminate, nor abusers of themselves with mankind, nor thieves, nor drunkards, nor revilers, nor extortioners, shall inherit the kingdom of God. And such were some of you: but ye are washed, but ye are sanctified, but ye are justified in the name of the Lord Jesus, and by the Spirit of our God." (I Corinthians 6:9-11 KJV). Jesus died to set us free from the crippled state the devil wants to trap us in. "If we confess our sins He is faithful and just to forgive us our sins and to cleanse us from all unrighteousness." (I John 1:9 KJV).

Healing Can Be Yours

Perhaps as you are reading this book, you can identify closely with some of the examples I have given. You really want to be healed in your crippled sexuality. Remember that, when Jesus walked on this earth, some of the people he healed were crippled in their sexuality. Mary Magdalene was a prostitute. May I suggest you share in this prayer with me, the same prayer I use during seminars on this subject:

Pray with me: "Jesus, thank you for my sexuality. I give it back to you, Lord. Please cleanse my sexuality and wash it clean. Take away all the hurt in me, and all the bad memories. Cleanse my thoughts. Make me a whole sexual person. Take away all of the crippling. I want to be whole. Now, Lord, please fill my sexuality with your presence. You said my sexuality is part of my body, and you said my body is a temple of the Holy Ghost. Lord, fill my sexuality with your Holy Spirit. Fill my manhood (or my womanhood) with your Holy Spirit. Fill my sexuality with your very nature and with your love. Make me the man (or the woman) you have planned me to be. Lord, let your love flow through my sexuality. From this time onward it will be the creative force that you planned it to be. In Jesus' name, Amen."

Principles
For Healthy Relationships

If you have developed the habit of expressing your sexuality outside of God's rules, God can heal you. This is what you must do:

1) Face your actions as sin, and confess your sin to God (Romans 10:9,10).
2) Ask God to forgive you (I John 1:9).
3) Give your sexuality to Jesus. He gave it to you; now give it back to Him.
4) Ask Jesus to cleanse your sexuality, to wash it clean and to break all the old bonds and habits of sin (Romans 12:1).
5) Your body is the temple of the Holy Ghost. Your sexuality is part of your body. Ask God to fill your sexuality with His Holy Spirit (I Corinthians 6:19).
6) Ask God the Holy Spirit to fill your sexuality with the very nature of Christ, and to fill it with the Love of God (Romans 5:5).
7) Ask God to use your sexuality to bond you to your partner, and to bless your marriage partner with the Love of Jesus as it flows through you in those beautiful intimate times when you are together.

For Further Study of the Scriptures from this Chapter

Proverbs 5	I John 1:9
Proverbs 6:32	Romans 10:9-10
I Corinthians 6:9-11, 13, 19	Romans 10:9-10
Deuteronomy 17:17	Psalm 38:11

Chapter Eight

"God Gave Them Over"

In this brief chapter, we will consider one key passage which will help us to clearly understand how our society — and we as individuals — has gotten to the place in which we find ourselves:

"Because that which may be known of God is manifest in them; for God hath shewed it unto them. For the invisible things of Him from the creation of the world are clearly seen, being understood by the things that are made, even His eternal power and Godhead; so that they are without excuse: Because that, when they knew God, they glorified Him not as God, neither were thankful; but became vain in their imaginations, and their foolish heart was darkened. Professing themselves to be wise, they became fools, and changed the glory of the uncorruptible God into an image made like to corruptible man, and to birds, and four-footed beasts, and creeping things. Wherefore God also gave them up to uncleanness through the lusts of their own hearts, to dishonour their own bodies between themselves: who changed the truth of God into a lie, and worshipped and served the creature more than the Creator, who is blessed for ever. Amen.

"For this cause God gave them up unto vile affections: for even their women did change the natural use into that which is against nature: and likewise also the men, leaving the natural use of the woman, burned in their lust toward one another; men with men working that which is unseemly, and receiving in themselves that recompence of their error which was meet.

"And even as they did not like to retain God in their knowledge, God gave them over to a reprobate mind, to do those

139

things which are not convenient; being filled with all unright-
ousness, fornication, wickedness, covetousness, malicious-
ness; full of envy, murder, debate, deceit, malignity; whisper-
ers, backbiters, haters of God, despiteful, proud, boasters, in-
ventors of evil things, disobedient to parents, without understanding, covenant breakers, without natural affection, implac-
able, unmerciful: who knowing the judgment of God, that they
which commit such things are worthy of death, not only do the
same, but have pleasure in them that do them" (Romans 1:19-
32 KJV).

What a fearful phrase: "God gave them up". Yet this is an
accurate description of so many in our world today. It is not that
God no longer loves this people; instead, He has simply allowed them to go the way they have chosen to go: deep into rebellion, sin and depravity.

Current Explanation

This accounts for much we see around us today. And we
must understand these things if we are to be able to fully com-
prehend how to have a fulfilling sex relationship, how to know
one another, and what kinds of crippling needs should be dealt
with.

If people are crippled sexually, they can undoubtedly be
found somewhere in this Romans passage. Sexual cripples will
usually try all manner of weird things, but they will never find
fulfillment. They will always be seeking a new gimmick. They
beat one another as part of the sex act. There are homosexuals
who shove steel rods up one another's rectums. This is sexual
freedom?

But let me stress: these people need God, they do not need
your hatred. I share these things simply to indicate the kind of
bondage these people are in.

I talked recently to a psychiatrist who worked with convicted rapists. He was not a believer. He told me, "I shudder at
the pornography, associated with violence, that is coming out
now." He went on to tell me what it is that makes a rapist: "He is
really a man who is angry at women. He is usually raised by a
domineering mother, or for one reason or another he is angry at
his mother. When he reaches the age of puberty, he begins to get

140

mixed up with pornography. He starts to take his hate out on girls, and he associates his sexuality with making the girl suffer. He has a few experiences like this, at the same time as he is becoming preoccupied with violent pornography which often focuses on rape. By the time I get to them they are usually 20 or 21 and it is too late."

I asked him about the practice of teaching women to defend themselves physically against a rapist. He said, "It is a good way to get her killed, because the only reason he is raping her is because he is angry at her. If she fights back, he will kill her. The devil strives to cause women to fight men and men to fight women, because that totally destroys love.

God Loves You And So Do I

I heard a story of a Christian woman in Toronto who was attacked in a back alley. A man jumped out of the shadows and began to tear her clothes off to rape her. She looked him straight in the face and said, "I love you. God loves you and I love you." He stopped in his tracks and began to cry. You see, she had confused his reason for raping her. If she had lashed out and scratched and hit him, she would have confirmed his antagonism, and she would have been raped.

There is no question that men have been enormously unfair in their treatment of women. But I believe that teaching women to fight back aggressively only aggravates the problem. Deep inside a man is a conviction that he is not supposed to fight a woman. That means, when a woman is aggressive, a man will usually turn and leave. Men are walking away from women in droves. They refuse to be husbands and fathers. Some men, who have been crippled in their sexuality, rise up and put the woman down with force. He beats his wife. Either way, everybody loses.

Look at that passage in Romans again. It tells us that every person has a knowledge of God, simply from creation. We are without excuse if we turn from that knowledge. If you really want to know God, you will find Him. The verses tell us that we stopped worshipping God, and began to worship man. That is secular humanism: there is no God, there is just man. For a full explanation, see Tim LaHaye's *The Battle For The Mind*,.

And then Paul tells us that God has given them over to a reprobate mind. Remember what we have said earlier: sexuality begins in the mind. Our minds are crippled, sexually. In place of love and commitment and faithfulness, there is hate and mercilessness.

But I write this book to tell you that, no matter what mess you are in, God can heal and restore. God can make you wonderfully free.

Principles
For Healthy Relationships

Fill your mind full of Scriptures, reading material and information that agree with God's principles. Stop using pornography and bad television because you are establishing a new habit pattern, not trying to feed the old, destruction pattern. If you slip, repeat the processes that are noted in earlier chapters.

For Further Study Of The Scriptures From This Chapter:

Romans 1:19-32

142

Chapter Nine

Sexual Needs Of
A Man And A Woman

Now about those questions you asked in your last letter: my answer is that if you do not marry, it is good. But usually it is best to be married, each man having his own wife, and each woman having her own husband, because otherwise you might fall back into sin.

"The man should give his wife all that is her right as a married woman, and the wife should do the same for her husband: for a girl who marries no longer has full rights to her own body, for her husband then has rights to it, too; and in the same way the husband no longer has full right to his own body, for it belongs also to his wife. So do not refuse these rights to each other. The only exception to this rule would be the agreement of both husband and wife to refrain from the rights of marriage for a limited time, so that they can give themselves more completely to prayer. Afterwards, they should come together again so that Satan won't be able to tempt them because of their lack of self-control" (I Corinthians 7:1-5 Living Bible).

As we have already learned, God's plan for our sexuality is holy and pure and without sin, in the context of marriage. It is beautiful in God's eyes. Christians who think there is something dirty about sex are wrong, according to the Bible.

Meeting Needs

According to the passage from Paul's first letter to the Corinthians, both the man and the woman have intimate needs. This is perhaps best described as the need to share your total intimate self with a member of the opposite sex, in a life-long relationship. Not only does Paul acknowledge these needs, but he instructs husband and wife to meet one another's needs. This is not just the wife meeting the husband's needs, but a completely mutual relationship.

"Grit Your Teeth And Get It Over With"

I have heard some crazy advice that is given to young girls who are about to be married. They are told that men have certain needs, and the woman must fulfill them. Therefore, the best thing the girls can do is to make up their minds to go through with it, and if they think about something else, it will soon be over. Oh God help us! The Bible makes it very clear that sexual fulfillment is just as needful for the woman as it is for the man. However, the woman is very different from the man, and her needs are not as readily apparent.

Some women go through their entire marriage without ever having their needs met. This is a shame. The Bible says that both men and women have a real need to share their sexuality intimately with their partner. And as we have read elsewhere in the scriptures, it is God's plan that sexual union should be one of life's most pleasurable experiences, both for the man and for the woman. God knew that eating food was necessary, but in His grace He also made it pleasurable. Not too many people feel that eating or enjoying food is sinful! Of course, misuse of eating is wrong, just as misuse of sexuality is wrong. But like eating, God has designed sex to be both a drive in us, and a joy for us. The devil did not invent sex as a temptation; it is God's gift. The most the devil can do — and he is being terribly successful in our day — is to corrupt and cripple our sexuality.

If we are to fully enjoy our sexuality, within the proper context of marriage, we need to understand the difference between a man's needs and a woman's needs. We need to learn to understand one another. We need to realize that at times we hurt one another without even realizing it.

A Man's Needs

Let's start with my group: the man.

A man has a stronger surface sex drive than a woman. God has made him to be the initiator. Now, it is not wrong for the woman to initiate sex, but God has made a man so that his drive is very much more on the surface.

When a man takes his wife in his arms and sexually makes love to her, it means, to him, "This is the most beautiful, intimate experience I will ever have with my wife. I am loving her. We will never be closer than we are right now. I am sharing my manhood with her." Usually when a man wants to love his wife, he thinks in terms of taking her to bed and sexually making love to her.

A Woman's Needs

It does not mean that to a woman. It is important that men understand this. Men, you must realize that the most beautiful, intimate, loving experience for a woman occurs when you take her in your arms and hold her, without sexual intercourse, and speak kindly to her and listen to her as she speaks of things that are really important to her. You talk and plan together.

This can be even more special if you are out together in some romantic setting, perhaps a restaurant. And then you come home, and hold her, and talk. To her this is the most beautiful, loving, intimate time in the world. It means that she is being loved. I can just hear the men saying, "Why did God play such a dirty trick like that, and make us so different?" Let me assure you — He knows what He is doing! That kind of loving, where you hold one another and communicate, is very good for you, men. In fact, you need it just as much as she does! God made women that way because the women bear the children, and God wants them to bear children to men who will be there for them! Their men need to know their concerns; they need to cherish their women and nurture them.

Common-law relationships and overnight affairs devastate a woman. She needs the commitment and daily communication with a husband. She needs the assurance of his tender presence. If she has that, then her body comes alive, and she enjoys her sexuality. She enjoys sexual union with her husband. Happy is the man who knows this, and who realizes that mutual fulfillment comes no other way.

Perhaps this will sound familiar: a couple has a fight. When the disagreement is over, they both want to make up. So the husband makes sexual advances, and wants to go to bed. She's not ready for that; she can't and she resists, and he accuses her of carrying a grudge, of refusing to forgive. He gets

145

upset. This entire problem is rooted in a failure to understand one another. By the way, gentlemen, if she does go ahead just because you want her to, to keep you from being upset, she will feel like a prostitute. God has not created her to give in to a man who has just bawled her out.

Men's Neglect

Far too often, a man will neglect his wife in these loving intimate areas. He gets too busy. There is, in the man, a genuine drive to earn a living. He receives his self esteem through providing for the family. However, he is often too occupied in business. How many businessmen work 16 hours a day, come home, want to make love to their wives, and instantly fall asleep? Before long, she isn't interested in that kind of quickie sex, and she'll turn him down.

Sexual Rejection

Rejection in the bedroom is devastating to a man. Because he sees this as the ultimate expression of love, he feels that his love is being rejected. He will feel rejected if he is turned down; he will also feel rejected if he realizes that his wife is not enjoying sex with him. He will feel that he has failed as a man. Women should realize that a man gets most of his pleasure from giving pleasure to his wife. That is what makes him feel good about his manhood. This is completely opposite to what most women believe, that men are only interested in sex for themselves. This means that if a woman communicates that she is just giving in, and having sex, to give him pleasure, he feels like a rotten pig.

After a wife has turned down her husband a few times, or has said something like, "Oh, go ahead if you really have to," the man not only feels rejected, but he also feels angry. The wife will hear the anger in his tone of voice, and then in his actual remarks. He will probably accuse her of being frigid. That will guarantee that she will be unable to respond. She is already neglected, and now she is feeling alienated and unloved.

By now, she is thinking, "Why doesn't he love me? All he wants is sex!"

And by now, he is thinking, "Why doesn't she love me? Doesn't she know how hard I work? She should be thankful to
146

have a husband like me." The more he feels rejection, the more comments he will make against her. The more comments he makes, the less she will be able to respond.

If this continues, it can be a very real danger to your home. You need to read the warning signals. If your wife is turning you down in the bedroom, you need to take her out for a romantic evening, or coffee and sharing together. You have probably been working too hard; you have certainly been neglecting her in other ways. You need to sit down with her and listen to her. You need to renew your loving relationship in other areas. If she is having trouble responding it is either because she is worried about something and hasn't shared it with you, or she feels neglected by you and does not feel like she is a part of your life.

Passed-on Problems

These problems could be greatly magnified if she had a father who was never at home, and who misused her mother. She might be very sensitive in that area and need a lot of that other type of love before her sexuality can respond.

The same can be true of men; I have known men who were impotent simply because they would not forgive their mother. It spills over to women in general. Sometimes a man who is angry with his mother will deny his wife her orgasms. Anger against a mother or a father can lead to homosexuality or lesbianism. We need to recognize these things; and then to allow God to deal with them and heal us!

Men: it is good for you to learn how to love her properly.

As we attempt to understand the difference between men and women, we must also realize that sexual union is man's greatest experience of pleasure. Usually, a man will put up with a lot of other things from his wife, but he will have a very difficult time coping if there is nothing happening in the sexual area. But if a man is regularly having satisfying sexual experiences, he feels better about all of life. He will go out into the world and find that the challenges he faces seem small. He can do anything — because he is loved. He is a success as a man, at home.

A man who is sexually satisfied will be a better leader at home. It will be much easier for him to be loving in other ways.

147

It will be easier for him to be kind to his wife and sympathetic to his children; in fact, to assume all of the appropriate manly duties. In general, it causes his manhood to come alive. In fact, ladies, if your husband loses his job or doesn't get the raise he wanted, counsellors recommend that the best thing for a wife to do is to take that man to bed and make love to him, and then tell him what a beautiful man he is and how she enjoyed it. He will be much more able to deal with the problem after that! And he will be a lot less likely to have ulcers, or high blood pressure, or any of the other diseases that are caused by stress and tension.

But remember: this only works for you if it takes place within marriage. A promiscuous lifestyle has the opposite affect; it causes a great deal of tension.

A Woman's Sexuality

A woman's sexuality is far more complicated than a man's. Some women go all through their lives without having a fulfilling sexual experience. This is unfortunate, because when a woman has a fulfilling sexual relationship within marriage, she seldom has nervous problems. A fulfilling sexual relationship allows her to be at peace with the world. However, if she is participating in the act, but there is no sexual fulfillment, no orgasm, no release, it does the opposite to her. It causes tension and frustration. She will not sleep well.

You can see that it is very important that the husband meet the wife's needs, and the wife meet the husband's. Therefore, the husband should concentrate on providing the most pleasurable experience possible for his wife; and the wife should concentrate on providing the most pleasurable experience possible for her husband.

Perhaps you are reading this and thinking, "I should show this to my wife so she can meet my needs." If so, you have missed the point! This message is for you. You need to be thinking of her, not of yourself, or you will never have a mutually fulfilling sexual relationship.

Loving Without Sex

There is another potential advantage that comes from taking the time to love your wife in the way she most responds to.
148

There are times in a marriage when it is impossible to have sex, and if sex has been the sum total of your "loving" relationship, you will find yourself confused about how to relate together. But if you have been sensitive to one another in the past, you will be much more ready to face such a circumstance. I have known married couples who were unable to have sex for long periods of time because of illness, but who maintained a strong, loving marriage. They have learned to be intimate and loving in other ways besides intercourse.

Some people participate in sex out of fear: they are afraid if they don't meet their partner's need, he or she will leave them. This is not right. You should participate in sex because it is a beautiful expression of intimacy, and a time of blessing your partner, not trying to manipulate them to make them stay. Besides, you cannot keep your partner; they stay from their free will. You do not remain in a marriage because you are forced to, but because of loving commitment.

Sight And Touch

Another difference between men and women is that a man is aroused by sight. If a man looks at his wife's body, he will be very quickly aroused. This can lead to a very simple disagreement in the bedroom: the husband may want to have the lights on, while the wife likes the romantic touch of low lights or darkness. The man is saying, "Let me look at you."

Remember the passages from the Song of Solomon? He is looking at her; she is saying, "Keep talking, keep telling me you love me."

The world concentrates much of its marketing on corruption of this truth. They sell pornographic magazines to men. Oh, I know they try to do the same to women, but I believe that most people that buy those "women's" magazines with sexual pictures of men, are homosexuals!

A woman can look at a man's body, and while she may be interested, it will not turn her on sexually. Men need to understand that. When men say to me, "She's not interested in my body," I answer, "Big deal. My wife isn't interested in looking at mine, either."

Why is this? God has made man to be the pursuer. He sees, and that turns him on, and he becomes aggressive. A woman is not aroused by sight. A woman is aroused by a man who is talking kindly to her, by a gentle loving touch, by caresses, by expressions of love, by closeness. It takes a long time to get her motor going. Happy is the man who is patient enough to wait!

A wife's sexuality is like a gentle spring flower waiting for the sun to shine on it. Gradually it opens when it feels the warmth. Let the warmth of your love shine for a while, and your wife will respond. There is no need to hurry. It is very important that the man learn and become skilled at meeting his wife's needs.

I believe that when a couple who understand and seek to meet each other's needs take the time necessary for fulfillment, it is the woman who receives the most pleasure. And I think this is fair because she bears the children. A woman can have two or three orgasms one right after the other. A man only has one.

Vulnerability

We need to understand that when a woman gives herself sexually, she makes herself completely vulnerable. She gives her whole self. At times, a woman cannot give herself completely because of physical circumstances — the children are in the next room, or the neighbours are noisy in the next apartment. A man is not nearly as sensitive to these things.

I tell you this to help you understand the differences between you and your partner. Often, the husband will become upset that the wife has allowed herself to be distracted, when in reality, it is normal.

Called To Meet Her Needs

Men, have you ever thought about sex as your calling? Well, God has called you to meet your wife's needs, not only to satisfy yourselves. If you have not been meeting your wife's needs, then the Bible says you are "defrauding" her. You need to learn what makes your wife tick. If she is continually meeting your needs, but never having her needs met, she will become very agitated, and she will make you pay in other areas. She

150

will complain about everything, she won't sleep well at night, and she will be basically unhappy.

Before it gets to that point, learn to care for your wife!

Birth Control

It is important to discuss birth control. The Bible does not teach against the use of birth control. There is a story in Genesis 38 about a man who used birth control to prevent a pregnancy, and they were severely punished by God. Some use this to say that God opposes birth control. But the sin in this story was disobedience against another law of God; it had nothing to do with birth control. He was using birth control after he was told to have a child.

It is very clear in scripture that sexuality is for much more than having children. Many times, God blesses us with children, but He doesn't force anything on us against our will. The problem is that some birth control methods do real damage to a woman's body, or cause early abortions. And sometimes operations are not good for a man, either.

The method I recommend is called the ovulation method. It is not 100 per cent sure, but it is safe and very natural. There are seminars offered to teach this method, and I recommend them very highly.

I do not recommend the birth control pill. It can be harmful to a woman's body. It can make women vulnerable to cancer. It inhibits a woman sexually, because it shrinks her ovaries. It can cause nervousness and agitation. This is not always the case, but it seems to me to be a large risk to take.

Let me go farther on this issue of birth control: I do not believe that God wants you to have all the children you can have, unless He especially calls you to that! I suggest that you pray together for God's guidance regarding birth control. He will guide you, and He will prepare you to have children when it is time. You will have real peace in this matter.

However, if a couple insists that they do not want to have any children, this may indicate a problem. If a woman cannot stand the thought of having a child, she will pull away from her womanhood and from her sexuality and therefore from her husband. A great many women are doing this today. The same is true of husbands. This will cause a lot of trouble in a marriage. There is a deep root problem here, and a person with this problem very much needs inner healing.

This rejection of parenting stems from a false belief concerning the entire question of being a husband and wife, a mother and a father. You cannot deny such a thing without denying your whole role as a man or a woman.

Successful Sex Therapy

Let me recommend an extremely successful sex therapy to you. I suggest this in seminars, and to couples I counsel. And the great thing about it is, it is free!

Here it is: Husband and wife, pray together before you go to bed. Ask God to bless your womanhood and your manhood. Thank God for each other. Then, go to bed and love each other.

What you are doing, when you pray together, is asking Jesus to be there, and to make that relationship what He planned it to be. It is a beautiful act of worship to the Lord, and a blessing to each other, and it is very important that both of you look at your union that way.

Here are a couple of examples of the kind of situations which can arise to trouble our relationships.

Sometimes, at the beginning of a marriage, if a young girl is a virgin, it may take a month before she experiences her first orgasm. I remember counselling one young couple who had been married for longer than that, but the wife was finding very little pleasure in their sexual union. Her husband was beginning to believe he was deformed, or incapable of satisfying her. As I talked to them, I began to share about the need for foreplay, for tenderness from the husband to the wife. I recommended a book concerning these things, and I shared the kind of issues I have discussed in this chapter.

I told them to read the book Intended for Pleasure by Dr. Wheat and I said, "In about three weeks' time, I want you to go to Niagara Falls for the weekend." I told the husband to concentrate on giving his wife her first pleasurable experience of sex. This should happen on the honeymoon, but most men are ig-

152

norant of the needs of their wives! Several weeks later, she came to me and whispered, "We had sex three times on the weekend, and it was wonderful." That is the way God planned it to be.

The Lord loves to bring relationships into balance and completeness. Many relationships are out of balance, and need the healing of God. Sometimes, people who have known little love in their lives want to make all of that up by constantly having sex. I knew a man who wanted it seven times a night! That is ridiculous — he was out of balance and needed to receive healing and love from the Lord.

A woman contacted me and said that she and her husband had a terrible sexual problem. Before she told me what it was, she said that she had been to three psychiatrists and psychologists and they had all told her to get a divorce, because staying with her husband would drive her insane. She had already had two nervous breakdowns and was in constant depression. She said, "I called you as a last resort."

When they were married, they did not know the Lord, but they had been saved two years later, and had been Christians for four years. In all that time, the only way they could have sex was if he got her drunk until she was unconscious. He would then have intercourse with her. They had two children from that method! They had participated in sex 12 times in six years. If he approached her any other time, she would literally vomit. That is how crippled she was in her sexuality.

I discovered that the seeds of this had been planted when she was very young. Her father was a very abrupt man who did not know much about love. Her mother was angry at him most of the time, and constantly told her that sex was a terrible, dirty thing and that men are terribly dirty. Her mother said that if any man approached her sexually, he was not loving her; he was acting in a wicked way.

If her mother ever caught her talking to a man, she would call her into the house immediately and keep her up until 2 a.m., calling her a whore and a slut and telling her how filthy she was. It was pounded into her that sexual experience was the dirtiest, filthiest thing in the world, and that any decent woman would never participate in that.

When she dated boys, if they kissed her she was horrified. In a couple of relationships, she flirted with them, reaching out for love, and then when they responded she would get angry. What had happened? The devil had lied to her through her mother, over and over again. I asked her to forgive her mother for lying, and to ask the Lord to heal her sexuality. In the name of Jesus I rebuked Satan and that lie, and I commanded her sexuality to be free from that lie, that her sexuality would no longer be crippled.

There are certain times in ministry that you feel a special anointing; this was one of them. I told the devil that he would not cripple this woman any more. The I read the Song of Solomon to her.

She said, "I didn't know that the Bible felt like that. I thought God hated our sexuality." I told her, "Tonight when you go to bed, I want you to give your sexuality to Jesus. I want you to tell Him to fill it with His very presence and His love. Use your sexuality to bless your husband with the very presence of Jesus. Let God bless your husband through your sexuality."

Her husband came home late that night and got into bed, and for the first time in their marriage she initated the experience and found it to be reasonably pleasurable. Her husband later said that he almost got up in the middle to turn on the light. He tought he had gotten into bed with the wrong woman!

A day or so later they had an argument and all the old feelings came back. She called me and said, "I was afraid that it wouldn't last, and it didn't. I'm feeling the same way again. I can't stand him to touch me. I can't even stand him to be near me." You see, breaking a crippling habit is like learning to walk. We take a few steps, and then fall, and take a few steps and fall again.

I ministered to her over the phone, and I called her and her husband in for a counselling session. He had some problems as well, which we began to deal with.

I found it necessary to call them every night at about 9 p.m. They would both be on the phone, and I would pray with them and minister to them and read some scriptures with them. I would lead her to give her sexuality to the Lord, and I would ask

154

God to bless their loving that night. They would go to bed and they would be fine. I got them into a pattern where they increased sexual activity to just about every night.

You see, you have to conquer a bad habit, in the name of Jesus. For two weeks I called them every day. Then I called them about twice a week. Finally I left it with them to call me if there were any problems.

A year later I talked to them, and things were going beautifully. The depression was gone from her. There was joy in that woman's heart.

The Crippler: Satan

You see, when the devil gets hold of your sexuality, he gains a hold as well on your soul and your spirit. He doesn't care how he cripples you, he just wants you to be crippled. He wants you to be a lesbian, or in a breaking marriage — he wants you to use your sexuality to hurt someone. He'll be satisfied as long as the love of Jesus is not flowing through you.

But God wants born again, spirit-filled husbands and wives to be loving each other, sexually. It was His idea in the first place! If there are some problems, God Himself will help you to sort them out. He will guide you in the most beautiful way.

Let me caution you: it is not wise to talk to other people about what happens in the privacy of your bedroom. Unless you need a counsellor, you should keep it between the two of you. The intimate experience between you and your partner is something that no one else should ever share. That special intimacy is rather nice, isn't it? Your relationship is unique to you.

The Lord, in His word, does not give a lot of advice with regard to activity in the marriage bed, but He does lay down the key principle: the husband is to concentrate on meeting his wife's needs, and the wife is to concentrate on meeting her husband's needs. Neither of them are to force on the other something that is unpleasant. A man who is crippled in his sexuality may associate hurting his wife with pleasure. But if you have a husband like that, you should seek help from a Christian counsellor, for your husband's own benefit. Wives should not use

155

their sexuality to manipulate their husbands. To do so is to become a prostitute — to sell yourself for favours!

Out in the world they are into a lot of "kinky" things, but it is my observation that people who have a complete love relationship in other areas do not need to experiment with a lot of kinky things. A lot of things can happen between a couple during foreplay, but I believe that all the foreplay should be towards the normal act.

Ask God to guide you. Pray together for the guidance of the Holy Spirit with regard to your foreplay and your intimacy. You may have never thought of this way, but don't you know that Jesus died and rose again that we might be whole and complete in all aspects of our lives? That includes completeness in God's gift of human sexuality!

Principles
For Healthy Relationships

Here is a questionnaire for each partner in a marriage to fill out, in order to help you in your communication. I recommend that the husband and the wife each fill out their section of the questionnaire. Then, exchange your answers with each other, and discuss your responses openly, and in love.

Answer the questions quickly, and honestly.

For The Wife:

(Answer these questions with "Yes", "Sometimes", or "No".)

1) Is your husband willing to openly discuss matters related to sex? _____
_____

2) Do you tell your husband what sexual activities do not appeal to you?
_____

3) Do you tell your husband what sexual activites do appeal to you?
_____

4) Have you and your husband discussed your feelings concerning birth control use and methods? _____

5) Do you have difficulty initating sex? _____

6) Do you and your husband agree concerning how often you make love?
_____

7) Do you and your husband discuss ways to improve your sexual relationship? _____

8) In your opinion, does your husband understand your sexual needs? _____

9) Does your husband ever complain that you do not understand his sexual needs? _____

10) Does your husband tell you of his sexual needs? _____

11) Are you and your husband physically affectionate? _____

12) Do you let your husband know when you would like some physical affection? _____

13) Would you find it difficult to accept suggestions from your husband concerning improvements to your sexual relationship? _____

14) Would your husband find it difficult to accept such suggestions from you? _____

15) Do you tell your husband when you have enjoyed making love? _____

16) Does your husband tell you when he has enjoyed making love? _____

17) Do you ask your husband to do things which you enjoy sexually? _____

18) Does your husband ask you to do things which he enjoys sexually? _____

19) Do you find it hard to tell your husband concerning what you enjoy, sexually? _____

(Fill in the blanks)

20) In terms of my sexuality, I'm _____

21) Talking with my husband about sex _____

22) Physically touching my husband _____

23) My husband and I enjoy _____

24) When my husband and I talk about sex, _____
_____

25) I wish _____

For The Husband:

(Answer these questions with "Yes", "Sometimes", or "No".)
1) Is your wife willing to openly discuss matters related to sex? _____

2) Do you tell your wife what sexual activities do not appeal to you? _____

3) Do you tell your wife what sexual activites do appeal to you? _____

4) Have you and your wife discussed your feelings concerning birth control use and methods? _____

5) Do you have difficulty initiating sex? _____

6) Do you and your wife agree concerning how often you make love? _____

7) Do you and your wife discuss ways to improve your sexual relationship? _____

8) In your opinion, does your wife understand your sexual needs? _____

9) Does your wife ever complain that you do not understand her sexual needs? _____

10) Does your wife tell you of her sexual needs? _____

11) Are you and your wife physically affectionate? _____

12) Do you let your wife know when you would like some physical affection? _____

13) Would you find it difficult to accept suggestions from your wife concerning improvements to your sexual relationship? _____

14) Would your wife find it difficult to accept such suggestions from you? _____

15) Do you tell your wife when you have enjoyed making love? _____

16) Does your wife tell you when she has enjoyed making love? _____

17) Do you ask your wife to do things which you enjoy sexually?

18) Does your wife ask you to do things which she enjoys sexually? _____

19) Do you find it hard to tell your wife concerning what you enjoy sexually? _____

(Fill in the blanks)

20) In terms of my sexuality, I'm _____

21) Talking with my wife about sex _____

22) Physically touching my wife _____

23) My wife and I enjoy _____

24) When my wife and I talk about sex, _____

25) I wish _____

For Further Study Of The Scriptures In This Chapter:

I Corinthians 7: 1-5   The Song of Solomon

Chapter Ten

Communication

"When a man hath taken a new wife, he shall not go out to war, neither shall he be charged with any business: but he shall be free at home one year, and shall cheer up his wife which he hath taken." (Deuteronomy 24:5 KJV).

Communication: How To Understand One Another

In this chapter, I will discuss communication — understanding one another. Most of the problems in a marriage come from a lack of understanding, the inability to communicate properly one to the other. You say one thing and your partner hears another. You try to fix that by saying something else, and he or she hears yet another thing. There is a misunderstanding, and you finally just shut up. Communication dies.

Fear

Do you know what happens to men and women? Fear.

As a man and woman plan to become married, they become very afraid. Then they get very excited about the wedding, and then they become frightened again. They look for all sorts of signs and hints: "Does he really love me?" and "When I'm at my worst will she still care?" Sometimes a spouse will actually, subconsciously, do the things that their partner doesn't like, so he or she can see the response.

This is why the Bible makes this very special rule about the first year of marriage. All kinds of emotions and questions come to the surface in that first year. This is an especially crucial time for the wife, because, as we have discussed, in order for her to truly relax and be comfortable in their relationship, she must feel that her husband really knows and loves her.

159

The Bible is very clear that when a girl becomes a wife, she has a period of adjustment. That is why the man is told to stay home and "cheer her up". Sometimes she will lash out at the smallest things, and then gush all over her husband. She will do things that seem very out of character. The husband may react by wondering "What's going on?" The Bible has the answer.

Not Even The Birds Are Unisex

The first year is spent in getting used to one another. In this, like almost everything else, there is a real difference between the needs of a man and a woman. Unisex is for the birds! The problems are not caused by these differences, but by our failure to understand these differences.

The musical asked, "Why can't a woman be more like a man?" Well, she can't. A woman's brain even functions differently from a man's. She thinks differently, and she reacts differently. Things are important to her that aren't important to a man, and vice versa. The reason for this is, God has a different purpose for a woman, as compared to a man. God has made both man and woman with a wonderful plan; He wants you to come together to fill the empty places in one another's lives. This could never happen if you were exactly the same: gears that were identical would grind, but gears that are opposite, mesh together!

Because you are different, you need to learn to understand one another.

The Man As Communication Leader

God calls men to take the lead in communication. Most of us don't, and this leaves most women frustrated. One of the most frequent complaints I hear from women is, "He won't talk to me." They say, "He comes home from work and he asks, 'What's for supper?', and he eats supper and then goes and sits in front of the TV." When she asks a question, he answers with a grunt, or with a word or two.

By refusing to communicate, you are shutting your wife out of your life. She needs to feel that she is sharing in every part of your life! As I have mentioned earlier, in Biblical times, the
160

husband and wife, and eventually the children, all worked together. Our society is not set up like this; and in our society, marriages are falling apart.

It is important that, every day, you share what you are thinking, and the new things that are happening in your life. I like to compare it to manna — it came every day, and you couldn't use yesterday's, because it spoiled after one day. Communication between a husband and a wife has to happen every day, as well.

"You husbands must be careful of your wives, being thoughtful of their needs and honoring them as the weaker sex." (I Peter 3:7a Living Bible). This simply means that women bear the children, and because they do there are times when they need protection and they need your understanding. But it certainly does not mean that they are inferior! Women are not as physically strong as men, but in other ways, a woman is much stronger than a man. She can stand more pain than a man.

That verse continues to read: "Remember that you and your wife are partners in God's blessings, and if you don't treat her as you should, your prayers will not get ready answers."

Men, have you been praying, but finding that God wasn't answering? This may be the reason. This is one reason I advise husbands and wives to pray together; you become partners in receiving God's blessings. When you talk it over with your wife, and pray together, you will be surprised at how quickly the answers come. Very often, a husband and wife who pray separately are actually praying for very different things for their family, because they have different priorities. God's will is that you would be one, as Jesus and the Father are one.

The Nest Syndrome

A key difference between women and men that men need to understand is the "nest syndrome". We have already encountered this, although not by this name. The woman needs to feel secure. She needs to feel that her man is committed to her. When she marries, she looks forward to the security of a home. She has a definite sense of how the furniture should be placed, and what colour of curtains they should have. It is of great importance to her that the house be just the way it should be.

This is so important that if a man does not take notice of these things, she feels as though she is not important to him; that he does not love her.

But the man is usually completely different. All that matters to him about the home is that he shares it with her! She is what is important, what makes it his home. He may like to have a nice home, but the details really don't matter a lot.

Sometimes the man tries to take over the function of decorating the home. I know of one case where the man bought the house, purchased all the furniture, had it delivered, and put it all in place. His wife came in and began to cry. Why? Because she wanted her own personality to be in that home; she wanted to prepare her own nest. But it wasn't hers; she had had no say in it.

Romance

A woman has a much greater need for romance than a man. God has created her in such a way that she will constantly look for little signs that you still love her and notice her. If you are 75 years old and she is 74, she'll still look for those signs.

A man does not react that way. When he becomes married, he begins to work harder, to be the provider. That is how he communicates his love for her: by providing for her and the family. But a woman needs to be assured of her husband's love in more detailed, intimate and romantic ways.

The Importance of Detail

The woman is always more concerned with detail than the man. Just think of what it is like when a baby is born to a couple. The man says, "What is it, a boy or a girl?" That is all he cares about at the moment. But the woman holds the baby and looks at every freckle and every dimple and every hair and every little toe and every little finger. She soon knows every bit of that baby. She cares about details. And this is wonderful, because the woman is much more sensitive to the child's emotional needs, far better equipped to be mother in the home.

Or think about your wedding. The groom just wants to get married, get this over, and get on with life. But to the bride, every single detail is important: her wedding dress, the colours of the bridesmaids' dresses, the flowers, the reception, the guest list, the details of the ceremony.

It isn't because the man cares less or the bride, more; it is because we are different, and therefore need to understand one another. That is why the groom must cooperate with the bride in the planning and the details, or he will ruin her special day.

And from then on, gentlemen, you had better remember that special day each year, or she will think that you don't love her. Remember, to a woman the details are important; if you don't think they are, she will believe that you don't think she is, either! When you remember the anniversary, and many other special occasions, you are telling her that you love her.

Just as she is a detailist in regard to your wedding day, she probably remembers every detail of your meeting, your dating, and your courtship. She remembers all the details of the birth of your children. Every now and again she will test you and ask you if you remember. An intelligent and loving husband will do everything he can to know these things, too.

Ladies, do not let anyone convince you that men are as well equipped as you to remember these things that are so important to you. They're not, any more than you are as well equipped to battle in the world as your husband is. God made you different!

Any society that has reversed the roles of men and women, has ceased to exist. Any culture in which women took the lead as worker and provider is gone. Reversing roles does not lead to freedom; it leads to extinction!

Everyday Details

This sense of the importance of details can also affect something as mundane as taking out the garbage. A wife asks her husband to take out the garbage on Tuesday, and he forgets. She reminds him, and he says he forgot, but he'll do it next week. And he forgets again. The third week, the wife takes the garbage out after he goes to work on Tuesday and walks right past those three garbage bags. And as she carries them to the curb, she thinks, "If he loved me, he would have taken the garbage out."

163

I wonder what percentage of arguments between husbands and wives start with the garbage?"

When he comes home, Tuesday night, she blasts him for something all together different, but she is really angry and feeling rejected because of those three garbage bags, and what his forgetfulness symbolizes in her mind.

Men, we need to learn how to love our wives by paying attention to the details that are important to her. We need to learn to communicate, and to recognize and meet her needs. And, guys, she needs you to take the garbage out. You may think it is a small deal, but when you remember to take it out she feels like you are taking care of her nest with her.

Careful Understanding

A couple is wise to take special care to be sure they understand each other. For example, a woman I know received a call from her husband, who said, "I'm going to be home for lunch today." What she thought and what he meant were unfortunately very different things. She thought it was a great time for a romantic dinner, just the two of them. She got out the best silverware, and some candles and made some soup that was his special favourite. And then, she waited. Noon came, and went. By 12:20 she was getting worried. At 12:25 he walked in with another man from the office, said, "Sorry I'm late. I'm glad you have set two places." And he ignored her through the rest of his business lunch.

What we have here, is a failure to communicate. This could have been remedied if either of them had been more detailed in their conversation. But what we also have here, is a need for more communication. The worst thing that could happen is if she clammed up about her hurt. Now, they need to talk it out, speaking the truth in love, and putting anger aside.

Stored-up anger will cripple a person or a relationship. Confessed anger, with the help of God, will help us to go on from a bad experience to greater mutual understanding, sensitivity and love.

A Place Of Rest

We also need to understand how a man tends to view his home: he sees it as a place of rest. Most men do so much for other people when they are out in the world that they come home to turn off their minds and their bodies. What the man really wants to do is to be at home with his wife and his kids, and to relax.

Now, because he is thinking this way, he begins to believe something that is not true: he begins to believe that he needs the television set, in order to relax. Sometimes, we need to put a shoe through the picture tube! What did men do throughout the centuries before television was invented?

It is easy to realize what problems can be created in this situation. The man comes home to relax, but the wife has saved up a whole day's worth of conversation for him. The last thing he wants to discuss is the dripping tap in the kitchen; but that is the most important thing on her mind, because she has had to listen to it for days!

She brings it up, several times, and then she suggests hiring a plumber. He says, "There's no need to call a plumber, I can fix that in 15 minutes." A week later, he still hasn't found the 15 minutes, and she believes that her wishes are totally unimportant to him — that he doesn't even care!

The next night, in the middle of supper, Billy from next door runs in, yelling: "Daddy's away and the tap is running full blast into the kitchen sink and Mom can't turn it off. We need help.". Guess what happens. He jumps up from the table, leaves half his supper on the plate, grabs his tools, runs next door, and 20 minutes later returns home, having fixed the neighbours' tap.

This is a common misunderstanding. Men tend to be ready to work outside the home, and eager to rest in the home. But as we do this, without sensitivity to our wives, we are communicating to them that we don't care about the home we share with them. Husbands need to get to know what is important to their wives, and to begin to meet their needs. Wives need to get to know what is important to their husbands, and to begin to meet their needs as well.

The Importance Of Thoughtful Giving

Let me also encourage you men, to show your wife that she is important through the sensitivity with which you buy gifts for her. She is looking to see if you know her well enough to buy her something she will like, something in her colours and her size. She wants to know if you really understand her, and have taken the time to know her. If you buy her something that is not in her size, that communicates to her that you don't know her very well. On the other hand, giving her a sensitively chosen present offers her proof that you understand her and that you are concerned for her.

Do you know what I do? I made some terrible blunders in this area when we were first married, so now I pay attention to my wife, and her likes and tastes; I shop carefully, taking enough time to be sure I am choosing wisely; and I actually ask God to guide me to buy something for her that she will really like. I like to buy my wife something that she isn't expecting, but which she will really like.

And when you watch your wife on your anniversary, or her birthday, or Christmas morning, you will soon know that she appreciates the thought and effort. Even a little card is so important, because of her need for consistent and continual communication of love on your part. And let me suggest, harking back to earlier principles, that you write the card telling your wife that you love her, and expressing appreciation for some of her good points.

Men: Be A Leader/Be A Listener

If I seem to be writing primarily to the man, it is because God wants you to take the initiative in this area of communication.

Of course, communication is not only how we express ourselves to our wives. Perhaps the most important aspect of communication is listening. We men really need to learn how to listen to our wives. So often they are trying to tell us they are hurting, and we don't even hear them. Perhaps all she says is, "I've had a rough day," but if you don't hear that, and follow it up by asking her about it and listening, both of you will have many more rough days!

166

You can accomplish so much by putting your arm around your wife and saying, "Honey, you've had a rough day, haven't you? I think we should go out for coffee and talk about it."

Often our wives are desperately reaching out for our understanding, and so often we completely miss the message. A woman called me in panic, saying "Mr. Shepherd, you've got to help me. My husband just walked out the door and I don't think he's going to come back. You've got to get him back for me."

She told me that they had been arguing over some small issue, but the argument had become hotter and hotter until she finally said, "I don't want to see you again. Get out of this house and don't ever come back." The guy took her at her word!

But do you know what she was really saying? She was saying, "I need to hear you express your commitment to me right now, in the middle of this mess." He could have answered, "Honey, I'll never leave you. We're having trouble right now, but I won't go. I love you." That's exactly what she wanted to hear. But because of failed communication in both directions, all she heard was the door slam.

Abraham And Sarah

This is not a new problem. Even Abraham, the man of faith, failed to listen to his wife, Sarah.

"And Sarah said unto Abram, Behold now, the Lord hath restrained me from bearing: I pray thee, go in unto my maid; it may be that I may obtain children by her. And Abram hearkened unto the voice of Sarah." (Genesis 16:2 KJV).

He may have hearkened to her voice, but he didn't really hear her. I often ask the ladies in my seminars if Sarah really wanted Abraham to sleep with her maid. They always tell me, "no", after they have thought it over for the first time.

Sarah was expressing depression because of her perception of her own failure. She was past bearing age and had not given her husband a child, despite the promise of God. She had spent many nights grieving over this. She was sure her husband was wishing he had married someone else, someone who would have given him children. She probably felt Abraham was blaming her for the apparent failure of the promise.

167

Many wives believe that they are standing in the way of good things that God could be giving to their husbands. And often, men communicate that very idea to their wives. But to do so is very wrong, and very unloving.

Sarah simply did what most women did: she told her husband to go, to see if he would stay. Abraham failed; he went. Sarah's heart was broken. We men do such dumb things. Do you know what Sarah was hoping Abraham would say? She was hoping Abraham would trust God, and say, "Listen Sarah, we are one, and God is still in charge. If He wants to fulfill His promise, He's going to have to perform a miracle involving both of us."

Sarah would have rejoiced: "What a man is mine; he's a man of faith and commitment." But Abraham fell flat on his face, a posture familiar to most of us who share his gender.

Problems Of Culture

There is another problem that exists between the man and the woman in many homes that has nothing to do with their sex; I am referring to the issue of culture. Many couples have been raised in two very different cultures, one from the other. And while they may look and sound the same, now, in truth their upbringing has planted a whole array of expectations and habits in their unconscious mind.

These unconscious "seeds" may never be discussed, but they certainly affect your feelings and your expectations. They even affect your vocabularies: words may have different meanings to a husband and a wife, with disastrous results.

Some cultural differences are greater than others; for example, a North American marrying an African or someone from the Middle East would have major cultural barriers to overcome. But two people from different families in the same city, with different cultural backgrounds, can none the less experience serious misunderstandings if communication is not maintained.

My wife was raised in a home where everything was very neat and tidy. I was not. Our home had eight children, my Mom was a great cook and she would welcome anybody in, at any time. We would troop into the house, throw our coats — and
168

the coats of our guests — over the bannister and drop our boots in the hall. We would wrestle in the living room. She was a great Mom, but keeping a neat house was not her top priority.

My wife came from a home where everything was in its place, down to the smallest ornament. The whole house was dusted every day. Every coat was on a hanger in the closet. Company were always planned for far in advance, and served the best silverware. No one dropped in, unannounced.

You can imagine what it was like after we were married. God has an interesting sense of humour. He often brings opposites together. He knew that I needed some cleaning up, and my wife needed some loosening up. But oh, that first year was hard! We could never agree on the proper place for boots, or for coats. She would get upset when I flopped down and lay on the chesterfield.

Dealing With Differences

The differences are not important. What is important, is how you react. I reacted badly. I tried to make her like me. But as we have discovered earlier in this book, changing your partner is never your responsibility; you must leave that to God. God used my wife and I to make each other into more balanced people, praise the Lord!

Marriage is a time for dying, dying to yourself and your selfishness. And marriage is a time for healing, as the intimate, close relationship brings things to the surface that, if we give them over to the Lord, God will heal. And marriage is a time to bring alive special areas of your life, as you are totally vulnerable to each other, and striving to be sensitive, one to the other.

Many people who remain single all of their lives become very particular about having things their own way. But it is not good to have everything your way. The best thing in the world is for you to be shaken out of your own way.

Talk!

That doesn't mean you should suffer in silence. You need to learn to talk freely, honestly and lovingly with your partner from day one of your relationship. As I have written earlier, I

169

encourage every couple to take at least 15 minutes each day to sit down together and talk about how you think and what you feel and what is important to you. This is vitally important in the first year of your marriage, and continues to be important all through your life together. Neither one trying to force change on the other to accommodate the way you think and feel. Those changes will come but only in an atmosphere of love and communication.

Principles
For Healthy Relationships

Communication is one vital key to a healthy relationship within a marriage. As I recommended earlier, be sure you spend 15 minutes each day talking and listening to each other. This is an important way in which we obey God's command: "Let all bitterness and wrath and anger and clamor and slander be put away from you, along with all malice. And be kind to one another, tenderhearted, forgiving each other, just as God in Christ also has forgiven you" (Ephesians 4:31-32 NASB)

A Communication Helper

In order to help you, as husband and wife, communicate with one another, I include the following questionnaires. Each spouse should fill out their own form, and then talk together about your answers.

For The Wife:

(Answer "Usually", "Sometimes", "Seldom" or "Never")

1) Do you and your husband discuss your work interests? _____

2) Do you and your husband discuss the handling of your family's income? _____

3) Do you and your husband argue about money? _____

4) Do you lose your temper when discussing a problem with your husband? _____

5) Are you able to express your true feelings to your husband? _____

6) Does your husband offer you support in your roles in life? _____

7) Do you listen to your husband? _____

8) Do you and your husband talk about things of mutual interest? _____

9) Do you and your husband share and discuss your personal problems together? _____

10) Do you pray together? _____

11) Do you feel that your husband is sensitive to your feelings? _____

12) Are you sensitive to your husband's feelings? _____

13) Do you admit to being wrong when you are wrong? _____

14) Do you pretend to be listening to your husband? _____

15) Are your conversations at meals pleasant and comfortable? _____

16) Do you point out your husband's faults to him? _____

17) Does your husband point out your faults to you? _____

18) Does your husband listen to you? _____

19) Does your husband compliment you? _____

20) Do you compliment your husband? _____

21) Do you help your husband understand you by telling him how you feel, react and think? _____

(Fill in the blanks)

22) Our relationship _____

23) Currently, our major problem is _____

24) About my husband, I am thankful for _____
_____

25) I could help our relationship by _____

For The Husband:

(Answer "Usually", "Sometimes", "Seldom" or "Never")

1) Do you and your wife discuss your work interests? _____

2) Do you and your wife discuss the handling of your family's income? _____

3) Do you and your wife argue about money? _____

4) Do you lose your temper when discussing a problem with your wife? _____

5) Are you able to express your true feelings to your wife? _____

6) Does your wife offer you support in your roles in life? _____

7) Do you listen to your wife? _____

8) Do you and your wife talk about things of mutual interest? _____

9) Do you and your wife share and discuss your personal problems together? _____

10) Do you pray together? _____

11) Do you feel that your wife is sensitive to your feelings _____

12) Are you sensitive to your wife's feelings? _____

13) Do you admit to being wrong when you are wrong? _____

14) Do you pretend to be listening to your wife? _____

15) Are your conversations at meals pleasant and comfortable? _____

16) Do you point out your wife's faults to her? _____

17) Does your wife point out your faults to you? _____

18) Does your wife listen to you? _____

19) Does your wife compliment you? _____

20) Do you compliment your wife? _____

21) Do you help your wife understand you by telling her how you feel, react and think? _____

(Fill in the blanks)

22) Our relationship _____

23) Currently, our major problem is _____

24) About my wife, I am thankful for _____
_____

25) I could help our relationship by _____

For Further Study Of The Scriptures From This Chapter:

Deuteronomy 24:5   Genesis 16:2
I Peter 3:7   Ephesians 4:31-32